PURBECK REVEALED

Ilay Cooper

james**pembroke**
● ● ● publishing

james**pembroke**
● ● ● publishing

Published and distributed
by James Pembroke Publishing
90 Walcot Street
Bath BA1 5BG

To order copies please telephone 07813 308416

ISBN: 0-9548176-0-5

Photography by Ilay Cooper
lllustrations by Juliet Haysom
Maps by Ilay Cooper and Juliet Haysom
Designed and typeset by Caroline Wollen
Edited by James Pembroke and Jonathan Wollen
Printed and bound in Great Britain by
Friary Press, Dorchester, Dorset.

CONTENTS

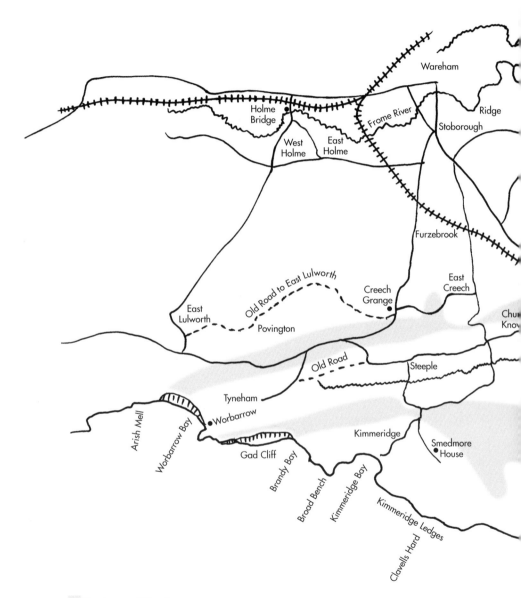

Denotes over 100 metres

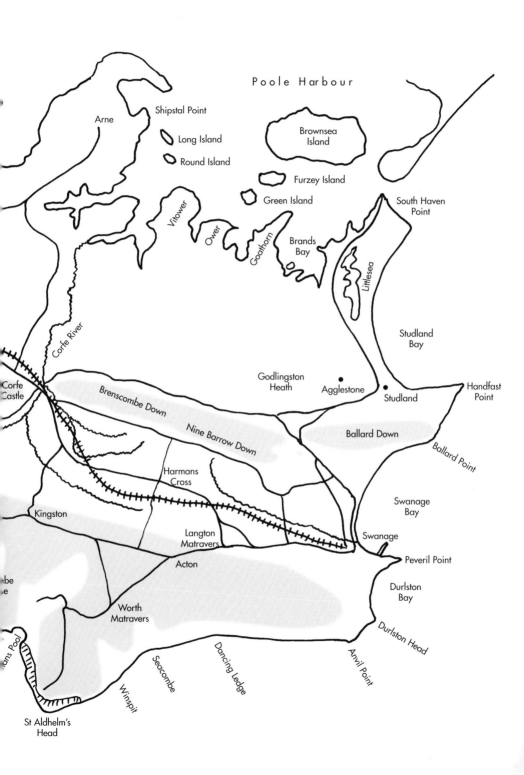

For Mary Spencer Watson

of Dunshay, sculptor

INTRODUCTION

'The Boundes of the said Islande goeth and dothe extende from a waye lyenge betwyxt Flowersbery and a wood called whitewaye and from thence to Ludgeford and from thence to Warham bridge and so still from thence by the sea syde toward the easte to a place called Studland Castle. And from thence contynially by the sea costes unto Sainct Aldomes chaple And so still be the sea coste westward untyll you come againe to the sayd place of Flowrysburye aforsaid.'

When Treswell defines his Purbeck on a 1586 map he also describes mine, home, a solid structure of earth and stone almost completely severed from the rest of Great Britain. I never planned to write about it. That is for other folk, viewing from a distance. I stick to Indian subjects. But James Pembroke, armed with a cheque, was persuasive. Admittedly I am well-placed. Purbeck has been home all my life. I was second of four lively kids, based until 1977 on 47 Ulwell Road. School meant Swanage: The Convent, Hillcrest and Swanage Grammar School; the last two now gone. Home as a structure has wandered but never as far as Corfe. I have managed to cling on despite the blight of urban wealth. There were intermissions: London for university, Paris to teach, long periods in the Indian subcontinent.

Most of my working life has been around Purbeck, too. Apart from the writing, there were jobs at Poole's BDH (British Drug Houses), on Brownsea Island, in the Grosvenor Hotel and, principally, at St Aldhelm's Quarry. As an appreciative country boy I explored the whole area; older, I still do. Many knew the facts, the history better than I: few have experienced as much of the island more fully. The streets, woods, cliffs have become events, moods, evocations. My parents took an interest in their surroundings, my mother in wild flowers, my father in birds. He owned the five-volume *Handbook of British Birds*, a first edition but of no value: it is far too well used. An interest in birds and the wish to see the next tract of land drew me ever further from home into the countryside. For kids there were no boundaries, only sharp eyes and the ability to run like hell.

When I read, it was birds, fantasy or of distant places. Never Purbeck. This book brought me fresh to a well-worn literature. Knowing the landscape, I could set the facts against it. It is difficult to avoid repetition. It is there. I can't ignore well-worn Corfe Castle, John the Bad, Brave Dame Mary. But beneath its shadow the stream turned scarlet when Richard Green stood on glass whilst catching eels. Along East Street, in the fifties Diddy Thomas could dribble a football from Townsend to school and only meet a single car. That is also Corfe.

I quote from Thomas Gerard's *Account of the County of Dorset*, written around 1620 but published by Coker a century later; Celia Fiennes' late 17th century travels recorded in notebooks discovered in 1885; Hutchins *History of Dorset* first published in 1774, the classic work; Philip Brannon's mid-19th century guide books; Charles Robinson's *Picturesque Rambles in the Isle of Purbeck* of 1882, even Gerald White's *A Walk from London to Land's End* of 1855. I refer to Treswell's 1586 map. There are other more obscure sources. I also draw on my diary - a date followed by a quote - which runs from January 1956.

An overriding interest in wildlife and the outdoor world motivated my choice of friends. 'We' punctuates the text. Some, such as Richard Dunham at Hillcrest, are fully named. Those few who appear throughout just get a Christian name. From the Grammar School came: 'Robert', Robert Smith, now returned from Oz to own Fordington Post Office; 'Richard', Richard Verge, who still owns Ulwell Farm. Robert, Richard and I wandered over Ballard Down, the Studland peninsula, the coast of Poole Harbour and Durlston's cliffs. Later, there was 'Trev', Treleven Haysom, who lived and lives in Langton. Now a master mason, he took over his father's business, St Aldhelm's Quarry. His definitive work on the Purbeck stone industry nears completion. 'We' most generally refers to him and I. Together we explored the cliffs and ventured into the army ranges. There was a third, 'Macky', Keith Macdonald, killed at Ballard at fourteen. He is not forgotten. Trev established an aged clinker-built boat at Chapmans Pool. 'John', John Pickford from Wareham, grew up knowing the northwest tract of Purbeck best. Much junior at school, he has just retired from a career in the BBC World Service. Youngest is 'Pete', Peter Du Cane (now with BP in Alaska) with whom I have been covering (for me revisiting) neglected tracts.

Seniormost, an invaluable source of information, is 'Mary', Mary Spencer Watson, sculptor, who spent summers at Studland from 1914 then settled at Dunshay in 1923. During the 1920s and 30s her family formed the nucleus of a creative circle in Purbeck and her work, spread widely across the country, includes *Purbeck Quarryman* outside Langton Church.

This is an individual, opinionated account. I don't purvey universal truths. At sixty-one, I look out through a sometimes jaundiced eye, hinting that the world of my youth was better. Is it youth or reality I regret? The kids of St George's School Langton and the rest of Purbeck are the future. Their world will leave me behind. I am happy with that, but why should I suppress criticisms? I hate the suburbanised countryside, all labelled, punctuated by warnings, crossed by wooden walkways. I hate manicured paths, stone- stepped; ugly CCTV intruding into birds' (and our) lives. I hate dangerous patrolling big-brother helicopters, roaring against the cliff, scaring birds and climbers alike; white status speedboats, the horrid buzz of intrusive jet skiis, unnecessary four-by-fours. I hate concrete gardens, profligate lighting, blind-eyed weekend cottages where once were homes. I hate the child-hood stolen from kids, the cars to and fro to school, the negative 'stranger danger'. I am sorry for those who never walk or cycle on a chore, always leap for their car. Why are they here? Clapham is more convenient and less muddy.

But I am the past. It is those kids' world now. It is for them to reclaim our mess. We grew up in a different world. I don't encourage a new generation to do as we did. We risked our lives climbing the cliffs and trees without ropes or helmets, swimming wherever we chose, taking rafts on lakes, trespassing everywhere, talking to anyone and venturing into the military area. Every year there were accidents, kids died. We were stupid, ignorant. I really ought to regret, but that stupidity is too deep-seated and the ignorance has gone.

★

My thanks are due to many people for help. I hope I haven't missed any. Firstly, Mary Spencer Watson, not only for information but for the loan of half her house for the book launch for which Charlie Newman gifted beer. Secondly, Treleven Haysom who read through and corrected an earlier draft. In addition my thanks are due to William & Hilary Bond, Dr Sue Brown, Dave Burt, Diana Campbell, George Carter, Bunny Farr, Nand Kishor and Sulochana Choudhary, Yogesh Choudhary, my father Allan 'Bill' Cooper, Jed Corbett, Peter Du Cane, James & Simon Goldsack, Bridget Kenward, Charles & Jenny McVeigh, Dr Philip Mansel (the pictures on pages ii and iii are courtesy him), Charlie Newman, Andrew Parsons & Alex Anderson, Roger Peers, John Pickford, Ravindra (Rabu) Sharma, Robert Smith, Richard Verge, Nicholas Warner, Peter White, Gwen Yarker, and the cooperation of the staff of Swanage and Dorchester Libraries and the County Records Office. I am also grateful to the advertisers, who have been generous when buying space at the back of this book.

The project needed a team. It could have been fraught: in fact it has been a pleasure. James Pembroke had the idea and published it. Josephine Pembroke chased after advertising and worked on the distribution. Juliet Haysom's drawings speak for themselves. Caroline Wollen has been responsible for design and layout. James Pembroke and Jonathan Wollen edited the text.

The profits of this book are destined for St George's First School, Langton Matravers: Juliet, like her father, Trev Haysom, was a pupil there; the Pembrokes and the Wollens have children there. I am grateful to them all.

ARISH MELL TO CHARNEL: THE LIBERATED COAST

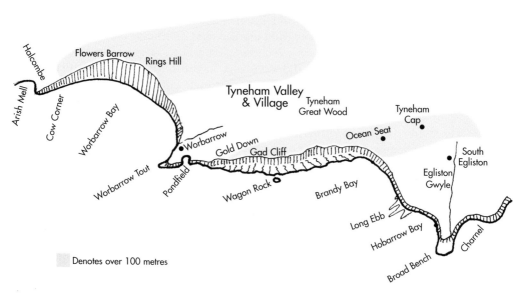

From Arish Mell to Charnel a strip of land running almost to the Frome River, within the Firing Range, was *terra incognita* when we were boys. It was all distant thudding, flashing gunfire and military exercises. The army took it in 1943 'for the duration of the war'. The frontier remains, marked by threats, red flags. This tract was saved from the fate of the rest of Purbeck. Here are no holiday cottages, well-sprayed fields, rows of lights. Weeds flourish amongst rusting shells. Wildlife prospers more happily under fire than in regulated sanctuaries. Fear of danger keeps folk clear.

The coast is Purbeck's most dramatic. The sea smashed through a limestone ridge joining Worbarrow Tout to Mupe Rocks, devouring the valley clays to form Mupe Bay. Confronted by the chalk it cut the high white cliffs of Cockpit Head and Rings Hill, exposing the spine of the Island, even ate through to form Arish Mell, where an ancient, ever-abrading stream carved a gap through the ridge. In geological terms the defences are down. A slight rise in sea-level, a few tumultuous storms and the sea will advance towards the Frome until Purbeck becomes an island in fact. A tiny bay, a nick in the cliffs, Arish Mell marks the traditional frontier, deriving its name from the same root as 'arse' coupled with the mill that may once have stood there. The hills rising east and west represent its stately buttocks.

I visited Arish Mell first long ago, stealing along thickets from the road with Trev, avoiding official eyes. From either side the coastal path pitches steeply down to that faint stream. Watercolours painted around 1900 show the bay innocent, a place for summer picnics, but now the beach, long host to the outflow of Winfrith Nuclear Power Station, is out of bounds. It is narrowly cut off from the shingle of Worbarrow Bay, the cliff projecting as a low chalk check. The alternative is Rings Hill, a long, steep descent down one buttock being paid for with an equally long, steep ascent up the other. This climb is softened by an odd curved dry valley. Its name, Halcombe, means a hollow valley. Above, truncated by the retreating crest of cliff, are the earthworks of Flowers Barrow, defence against one invasion, with below it a little concrete pillbox, sentinel against another.

Between the chalk of Rings Hill and the limestone of Worbarrow Tout are jumbled cliffs of easily-eroded Wealden clays and sands, the substance of the valley floor from here to Swanage Bay. They are colourful. Greens, yellows, reds, whites and greys intermingle with undergrowth.

To Thomas Gerard 'Warbarrow Bay' is 'so called from a Barrow now almost invironed with the Sea, which is not of anie Use...' Its shingle dips steeply into a clear tranquil sea. Turbulent when the prevailing wind is disturbed, each retreating wave tears noisily down to the depths. The name goes back at least to the 15th century and is said to imply a look-out, a role further stressed by the near-island hillock, Worbarrow Tout, for tout also means 'lookout'. Another, Hounstout, overlooks Chapmans Pool.

In 1957, our early teens, we first crossed the frontier and added the firing range to our territory. Once, thirty years back after a pollution incident, we came to Worbarrow at dawn looking for oiled birds, descending into the valley with polythene carrier bags to hold any victims. The beach was clean, neither oil nor birds, but it was scattered with packs of 200 cigarettes, crisps (which weren't) and 'aero' bars with brine in the holes. The 'crunchies' were good and the cigarettes had survived fairly well. Our empty bags were ready for them. The bounty spread along the beach to Kimmeridge. Soon after we had driven away, Customs and Excise closed the roads, searching cars. They had no warrant to search houses. To one householder they suspected of benefiting an officer remarked charitably 'I hope you die of cancer.'

As with most miracles, there was a logical solution on offer. A sailor in the bar of a train told me that supplies had been stacked ready for loading. Dockers went on strike and a gale blew everything into the sea. Others say that a helicopter's net broke as it carried supplies to a ship.

In the 19th century the coastguards took Worbarrow seriously. Smuggling flourished here into the 1840s and they had a lookout, a flag-staff and a pair of cosmetic cannon set up on the Tout. The coastguard station closed in 1912.

When we first intruded the shore-side cottages and all the other buildings in Tyneham valley stood as time left them. Some were vaguely intact but eyeless, many roofs had collapsed, ribs of rafters pushing through the tiles, walls ragged. The Miller family, of Scots descent, lived here by the shore, fishermen for generations, setting pots and nets. They were deeply involved in the smuggling along this coast. As the 19th century progressed and duties fell, the heiniousness and temptation of such crime reduced and with it the penalties. In the 1930s the Millers owned all but one of Worbarrow's fishing boats. Others of their breed supplied Celia Fiennes' meal on her visit to Tyneham, for she '...eat the best lobsters and crabs being boyled in sea water and scarcely cold, very large and sweet...'

The 16-year-old John Bond records another foraging foray from Worbarrow in his notes for June 1818. 'I went in a boat to shoot Puffins with White and my brother we landed at West Lulworth, dined at Red Lion Public House'. He bagged a large bird 'prettily streaked with black', a wagel, he calls it, consulting Thomas Bewick's *A History of British Birds*. That is a young black backed gull, then thought to be a separate species. He lost his new gun (worth £10) in 10ft of water where the bottom was rocky and weedy then ate the bird after washing it in vinegar, as he did all his kills. He found it good. White disagreed.

Almost a mile apart, Worbarrow was quite distinct from Tyneham, with its own shop. In 1911 a solicitor built a sympathetic, if badly posed stone house on the clifftop. Another family followed suit in 1921 with a hideous holiday pad, sharply conflicting with all about. The wreckage of both remained until the lead-up to regular weekend opening. Then ruins were demolished, manicured or made safe. Roofs were removed and walls tidied, creating their present severe, cement-topped finish.

The uncultivated scrub overlooking the bay is perfect for nightingales. Neglect favoured them because Lilian Bond, talking of neater times, comments on their absence from the valley. Driven from other parts of Purbeck, from the wildlife reserves intended to preserve them, now they are almost confined to the firing range.

The stream that drains Tyneham Valley empties into the bay. The nearby Tout, along with a submarine ledge running westwards from it, sheltered the fishermen's slipway, where their cottages stood. On the south, the Tout plunges as a Portland stone cliff, but the green hillock above is made up of

Purbeck beds, thin now towards the edge of the lagoon in which they were laid down. These show on either side, distorted here but not as gloriously as at Stair Hole. To the east is Pondfield, the little bay's name reminiscent of Punfield Cove, the north angle of Swanage Bay. Both share a thicket of reeds watered by a small but permanent spring. Amongst those reeds is a double line of defensive Second World War 'dragon's teeth'. All Mupe Bay, with the inshore waters to St Aldhelm's Head, falls inside Purbeck Marine Wildlife Reserve, set up in 1978. True to a new spirit of insensitivity, a warning notice was cemented into the Tout's dramatic rock surface.

The west end of Gad Cliff, sunk to its lowest point, feet in the sea, forms the east arm of Pondfield. Beyond, it rises as a fearsome line of projecting, jagged buttresses to a magnificent peak with a wedge-shaped head of rock. A gad was one of a set of steel wedges used by quarrymen to split block. Behind, Gold Down slopes back into Tyneham Valley with, arranged on its flank, static and mobile military targets. That 'Gold' and 'Gad' must be related. There was a 19th century coastguard lookout at the summit, a fine viewpoint from which I have twice seen a waterspout sail up the channel.

Beneath the massive limestone of Gad Cliff a layer of softer grey sands has been sculpted by the weather into hollows and bosses, its rugged surface undercutting the harder rock. Below again is a steep grassy slope formed from the Kimmeridge shales and clays which at its eastern end is extensive enough to nourish a little copse. Perhaps the army introduced the small herd of goats that have roamed wild there for some twenty-five years. Escape is easy but they seem content to confine themselves to the territory they were given. The shore is a mass of boulders, hard work to walk and climb over. Some are enormous, hurled down when the softer beds refused any longer to sustain them. The greatest, broken in two, is Wagon Rock, big and ancient enough to feature on walkers' maps.

At the western end the rocks give way to a short span of cliff falling sheer into the sea. Here only a few metres of water, a mere couple of strokes to swim, prevent crossing from that undercliff to Pondfield. Once in the chill of spring but keen to escape returning over those tedious rocks Trev swam it holding his clothes and binoculars above the water. He relaxed and they were soaked. While lying in the sun against the bank at Pondfield as his clothes dried he heard a landrover draw up. Officers, unseen and unseeing, stood above him, chatting. He held his breath, waiting to be discovered uncovered, until at last doors slammed and they drove off.

Eastwards the ragged wall of Portland stone retreats into the hill to be clad by sheep-cropped turf, forming a scarp running inland as Tyneham Cap and on towards Durlston Head as the southern ridge of Purbeck. Below, the shore turns away beneath grey shale cliffs crossed by a resilient limestone band, which slopes down to sea-level. There are several such conspicuous bands, each named for a feature it creates. This one becomes Long Ebb, a finger of rock gradually sinking below the waves as it projects out into the sea. Older maps mark the stretch of water thus enclosed as 'Tinham Bay'. That changed to Brandy Bay, first colloquially, in whispers, then openly. It is an isolated spot but in the angle between the limestone and the shale cliffs a path makes its way up from the beach, over the lip of the cliff, the ridge and straight into Tyneham village.

Fired by encouragingly high duties and despite excisemen, the brandy flowed in. Here it rested a while in the undercliff before crossing the ridge. The caches included a natural chamber covered by a huge rock, which survived into our time. Then the rock settled, crushing the space beneath. Now the path up the cliff is an overgrown route for badgers and deer, but then, when the coast was clear, the shipment would stagger up and over to Tyneham. Folk were sympathetic and many eyes watched for the excisemen. Not all consignments got through, however. Six men were caught on Gad Cliff in January 1834. Ranging in age from 16 to 34, they were sentenced to hang at Dorchester. Law moves with fashion. For its victims life, in full or part, is unrefundable. These men were lucky. The sentence was commuted to a year's hard labour. The judge no doubt drank their brandy.

As boys that was our first route into Tyneham valley. Seeing that cattle and sheep still safely grazed over much of the firing range unaware of the inherent dangers, we rationalised that, aware, we might carefully intrude. I never heard of an explosives accident on the Ranges. We would cycle to Kimmeridge, follow the beach then sneak over the exposed ridge near Ocean Seat, scanning the surroundings for the enemy. Once in the shelter of Tyneham Great Wood we were safe.

During the Second World War an RAF station overlooked Brandy Bay. To accommodate its personnel Ralph Bond quit Tyneham House for another, smaller. The station must have stood near where Ocean Seat remains, a little dry stone bower built by William Bond in the late 19th century, a sheltered place to sit and contemplate his good fortune. Me, I never pass it without thinking of my bad fortune, of two keys, long rusted away and useless, lost in the grass there. It was a sunny morning, winter announcing spring, thirty years ago and I lay back in the deep grass, ungrazed and uncut for hay, to savour its glory. Later, discovering those keys had fallen from my pocket, I went back but never found them. One opened the caravan, the other started my motorbike. I had duplicates, but consequences are unforeseen. Later that year as I travelled towards India on the motorbike a hair-crack in the key began to open. By Istanbul it was almost severed. A locksmith made a copy, but it was not quite good enough: he would finish it next morning. The bike spent that night in the porch of my hippie doss-house, the key so fragile that I left it in. The front wheel was free also since, locked, it would block the stairway. The manager assured me that the hotel was locked all night. He forgot Ramadan, the month of fasting from dawn to dusk. The doors would open well before dawn for the faithful to go out and eat. That bike went with them and I hitched the rest of the way. It was to be twenty-five years before Pete and I successfully biked that India road. Had I not lost the spare key...

Before ever rising up over the cliff-top into Tyneham Valley, and always more often than visiting it, we continued westwards along the undercliff or beside the shore. Here, amongst those great blocks of stone, an occasional boulder held pieces of crystal-veined fossilised tree trunk. The Portland Stone alters, narrows between St Aldhelm's Head where it is quarried and Gad where it never was. The best beds have faded out and hard chert devalues what remains. There were attempts to use it, a few fallen blocks showing tool marks, but it didn't repay the effort.

Those rocks are hostile, a powerful defence against landing. At only one place can a small boat nestle in to the shore. Once while landing I saw a regular pink shape through clear water. It was the phosphorbronze propeller

An Ammonite from the Kimmeridge Clay; the Gad Cliff propellor

which, discoloured, stands in the Square and Compass. Above that landing place was a hut, unshaped stone and driftwood, a ruin then, now almost vanished.

The cliff above, the most handsome stretch in Dorset, houses ravens and peregrines, struggling with each other as they struggled to survive when gamekeeper's poison killed the one and agricultural insecticides poisoned the other. We thought them doomed but now, poisoning stopped and dieldrin banned, both flourish. Cleared from the rest of Purbeck, here the ravens held on and to here the peregrines, although succumbing, returned. In 1985 they raised the first brood of young seen in Purbeck since we were kids. Buzzards held the tall trees at the east end of the undercliff and a kestrel, sharp winged and sharp voiced in ready defence, nested in the cliff beyond.

Weirdest are the cormorants, building on the lower levels where the weather has sculpted soft Portland sand into hollows and bosses. The colony at Gad Cliff, which was Purbeck's largest, has been outstripped by that at Ballard. At home in water, on the cliffs they become awkward prehistoric creatures, gurgling and groaning at their nests. The ravens harass them, one diving to scare off the sitting bird whilst the other comes in to grab the soft-green egg. Sometimes it stores the egg in a cranny, coming back for another. We would climb to the top of the steeply-sloping grassy undercliff, decorated in summer with glorious blue of viper's bugloss, and pass along below them in a narrow strip of soft grey dust and the stench of fish. The great cliff ran out above us, bright-eyed cormorants craning out over each sun-faded stick nest to watch. From the shore that shelf in the angle between concave cliff and convex undercliff looks simple enough, but it is intimidating, precarious. At fifteen we read *Henry V*: 'O'erhang and jutty its confounded base'. That is Gad.

The whole place was a secret world to us boys. We met no one. None of our contemporaries ventured that way. Yet years later Bill Langtry a decade older told me of venturing there with his mates, another generation of boys, in the late 1940s, raiding those precarious, deeply-groined lower levels for cormorants eggs. Between their time and ours a climate changed. Each spring they raided the nests, we counted them. My diary for 21st May 1978 mentions rowing from Chapmans Pool (it took two hours) and counting 83 nests from Wagon Rock, which gives a panorama. Year on year, they ranged between 60 to 100 nests.

Alone or in company sometimes I slept out on the soft turf above the landing place, waking to those ancient cormorant gobblings and groanings, the high fluting of the chicks. And, being the era it was, tripping on 'acid' on sunny days, looking up into the disordered sky, seeing sounds like contour lines fanning out from their focus, losing grip of day, of hour until brought to sense by the chill of dusk. Once when the sea became rough all-

unannounced during our fantasy travels, we were forced to sleep there unprepared. I was a waiter at the Grosvenor Hotel in Swanage, due to serve breakfast at 8 am. We set off at dawn but snagging a pot-rope, the propeller clip broke. I rowed in to Kimmeridge and, leaving Glyn to get the boat back to port, hitched to Swanage. I arrived, still uncertain of reality, in time to receive a tip almost equalling my weekly wage from some departing guests.

Beyond Long Ebb a rough beach, little Hobarrow Bay, curves to a great terrace of limestone, the same bed as Long Ebb faulted again to sea-level. This is Broad Bench where, given breeze, men on bright-sailed surf-boards set out to cross Kimmeridge Bay.

Nearby, a streamlet cutting a nick in the cliff has been halted by the limestone band, creating a little waterfall, fed by a spring from below the ridge. Its damp progress is followed by the trees and undergrowth of Egleston Gwyle, which belonged to the Grange Bonds. At South Egliston, the head of the Gwyle, Denis Bond, the late 18th century Rector of Steeple, built a house. In the mid 19th century French windows and a loggia were added and it became Lady Selina Bond's summer retreat. She, an Eldon, had married Nathaniel Bond of Grange. Lilian Bond calls Egliston a cottage, but its size and well-worked dressings indicate it was more than that.

When we discovered it the ceilings sagged, a barn owl lived in the roof and an upper room held an ancient hip-bath. Paving and roof tiles leaned against the façade beside a fire surround, broken as it was prised out. In spring snowdrops flowered early in its lost garden and as the year progressed other cultivated flowers fought their way up through the sturdy undergrowth. As the summer faded there were rich pickings from plum and apple trees.

To us it is always the damp grey ruin thick in ivy and shadow, sad in its lost garden, surrounded and hemmed in by brambles and trees, which we stumbled upon almost fifty years ago. Today, a yew contends with the engulfing thicket and in front of the cottage next door a stunted apple tree clings on, still blooming sparsely each spring.

In a sharply evocative watercolour of 1899 Leonora Bond captures another Egliston. Here, the house complete with loggia stands living in the sunshine. Her house has people indoors, unseen: they will pass. The gardens are bright with flowers, well tended, a creeper climbs the east wall. But the trees are there, waiting.

Later, Egleston was let to tenants savouring its isolation. Mary and her mother rode over from Dunshay in the late 1930s to stay with Ivy Bartholomew, a writer then in residence. She remembers the wooden shutters resembling those of Dunshay Manor, remembers their hostess as a late riser. They chose to set off early, leaving her to sleep. Whilst searching the cupboards for breakfast they chose the wrong jar. In place of tea they drank a powerful laxative, which caused many dismountings on the way. The Bonds planted some of the trees along the gwyle to shade them as they walked to and fro from the shore.

There is another ruin, Stickland's Cottage, towards the bottom of the Gwyle. Dead now, its Welsh slate roof falling in, Lilian Bond describes it as crowded with Louis Stickland's handicraft, beautifully finished furniture and model ships. The Sticklands had lived there several generations when the army came. They built small clinker boats and fished, had a boathouse at Charnel (Lilian writes both Sharnel and Sharnal). Why Charnel, with visions of torn cattle corpses, for an innocent grassy cut down to this baylet? Their boats grace the foreground of a view of Kimmeridge by Leonora's brother, John. Of a Sunday morning in the 1900s, Louis Stickland, an old man complete in black frockcoat and square-top hat would walk up over the ridge to Tyneham Church rather than patronise that of Kimmeridge on the rival Smedmore estate. Was his father William Stickland, 'aged inhabitant' of Tyneham, who died in 1881 having been in early life the leading spirit among smugglers? Certainly, his son, Will, continued the business until the evacuation.

The frontier is well-marked, heavily warned. Around the next headland is safety and the world of busy tourism in Kimmeridge Bay.

From Kimmeridge to Chapmans Pool

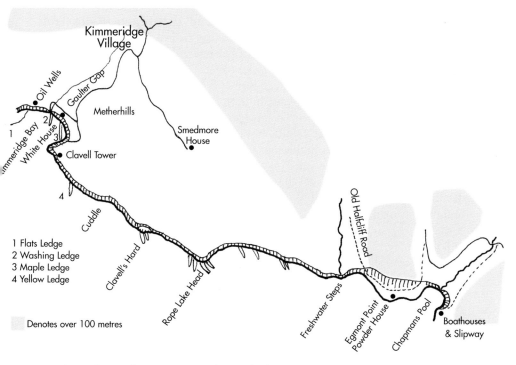

Kimmeridge Village

Oil Wells

Gaulter Gap

Metherhills

Smedmore House

Kimmeridge Bay

White House

Clavell Tower

Cuddle

Clavell's Hard

Rope Lake Head

Old Halfcliff Road

Freshwater Steps

Egmont Point Powder House

Chapmans Pool

Boathouses & Slipway

1 Flats Ledge
2 Washing Ledge
3 Maple Ledge
4 Yellow Ledge

Denotes over 100 metres

The military frontier coincides with that once dividing Bond lands from those of the Mansels of Smedmore. Kimmeridge and its surroundings belong to the Smedmore Estate. The much-altered 12th century village church (extensively rebuilt in 1872) and the parsonless Old Parsonage, built in 1837 so barely Victorian, are sheltered amongst trees beneath the grassy scarp. A row of handsome headstones stands west of the church, all similar, all to coastguards. Four are over men, each aged 26 when they died accidentally, probably while searching for smugglers. One, a boatman, died in January 1811, one was 'killed by his own firearms' in February 1841, another drowned on duty in April 1839 and the same year the fourth 'accidentally fell over the cliff' on an October night. That last could be foul play. The clifftop path was marked by whitewashed stones set at short intervals to help coastguards follow it at night. Smugglers would slightly shift those stones so that they led over the cliff. Amongst Kimmeridge smugglers were several Coopers (I claim no kinship), including Reuben, convicted 1821 aged 20, and 'disorderly' Charles, caught in 1840 when 27.

Near the old farmhouse, radically transformed in the 1830s, a footpath follows the stream down the gwyle. The road, descending past the drive to Smedmore House, turns sharply left through the straggling row of stone cottages to cross the flank of a hillock, Metherhills. Both head for the bay.

Sir William Clavell, of a family long settled at Barnston Manor, built Smedmore in the early 17th century, intending to live close to his business interests. The core of the building probably conceals an older house. Today it looks west, up the drive. It was designed to face the sun, the south elevation being Sir William's façade and seen from that quarter it harmonises with other 17th century Purbeck manor houses. Even that face is renewed, added in the early 18th century, and it is now concealed by the trees that enclose a pretty garden. The present façade, built in 1760, has a semicircular bay at either side. Seemingly too ponderous for the building, these bays create broad vistas from pleasantly-lit rooms.

The Mansels, holders of the manor for the past two hundred years, descend from Clavells and Wyots through the female line. William Wyot bought the manor from the de Smedmores in 1391. It has never been sold since. There was a hiccup, however, when eccentric Revd John Clavell died childless in 1833. Probably he intended to pass the estate to his steward, John Barnes. Major J.C. Mansel in his book *Kimmeridge and Smedmore* expresses honest doubt. Months after Clavell's death a will was found naming Barnes, but the family objected, declaring it forged. The case of Barnes vs Mansel of 19th May 1836 caused a stir in Purbeck. The judge found no evidence of the will having been signed... 'the court is bound to go further and to condemn John Barnes, the party, in the costs incurred.' That crippled him and he disappears from history. Certainly it seems odd that the old man should leave almost everything to an employee he had known for less than 18 months - but such things happen. The legal profession, well versed in criminality, closed ranks with the 'quality' and the estate passed to the closest descendant, Louisa Pleydell, a niece, who married a Col Mansel. Mrs Panton, in her lively, tactless book, says the family 'won by a fluke'. The margins of the Smedmore copy are richly annotated with 'No', 'Not accurate', 'False'.

At school, leafing through books on Dorset natural history, I grew very familiar with John Mansel-Pleydell. His 19th century work on birds, flowers and geology remains important. He had inherited Smedmore in 1863 but eight years later the estate of Whatcombe was left to him, conditional on his adopting the family name of Pleydell.

Dr Philip Mansel, remodelling the grounds to the west and southwest of the house, has set up a granite obelisk as the focus of one ride. It was one of a pair of giant gas lamps outside the church of St Mary Woolnoth (the other stands on Ballard Down) acquired by acquisitive George Burt and brought back as ballast aboard stone boats. I remember the Smedmore obelisk lying for decades beside the road at Sunnydale until the writer, Eric Newby, acquired it for Bucknowle House. Later he sold it to Smedmore.

The road to the sea forks near the hideous White House, built in 1936 by the Duke of Somerset on land bought from the estate and springing up before planning regulations condemned its like. Today, the main road veers sharply to the clifftop car park but the old track ran straight ahead, passing near the coastguard cottages on its way to the slipway. Beside the car park is Gaulter Gap, a little chine where both stream and path make their way to the shore, its name derived from 'gault', old English for grey clay. The row of cottages was built in the 1860s to house miners employed in one of several doomed attempts to exploit bituminous shale. It succumbed even before the miners moved in.

On the clifftop west of the cottages is Kimmeridge's most successful, least intrusive industrial enterprise, the first of Purbeck's onshore oil-wells. My diary for April 1959 mentions an 'oil pylon', the drilling rig. That was the year they struck oil. The inconspicuous nodding-donkey came afterwards, drawing on a reservoir in the Cornbrash, 560m down. It all seemed wonderful to us. Oil wells belonged in Texas, not here.

The most prominent feature on the Kimmeridge coast is Clavell's Tower, a folly built by Revd. John Clavell, last of that name and whose will caused so much trouble. Built in 1830, the fabric is of yellow stone taken from the beach below, pitched into shape and clad with cement. The rounded arches and windows are dressed with brick and Portland stone has been used for the decorative parapet and the colonnade which surrounds its base. Rarely used by the family, it passed to the coastguards as a lookout, their flagpole's stays attached to four small Napoleonic cannon set upright in the ground. By the mid 19th century such coastguard posts dotted the coast from Shell Bay to Worbarrow slowly to disappear as the charm of smuggling faded. Later, one cannon was sold, another stolen. The survivors, painted and set up on a carriage, guard the front door at Smedmore House.

A game elderly lady, Ione, told me that during the early years of the 20th century her grandfather rented the Tower for holidays. Later it deteriorated and by 1932 'the flooring of the different rooms is rotting away and one can only reach the top safely by keeping close to the walls.' Now all the floors are gone but Clavell's Tower, duly embellished but poorly disguised, achieved fame as The Black Tower of P.D. James' novel. Gradually the cliff line has retreated to threaten it. A Grade II listed building, Dr Mansel is gifting it to the Landmark Trust, which faces the challenge of moving it back from the abyss!

Along the shore east of the tower another calcareous band forms Yellow Ledge, projecting out to sea. Here the beach alternates between patches of shingle and tabular pieces of that yellow stone, fallen in an odd jigsaw as the soft shale erodes from beneath it. To the observant eye some beds of the shale reveal marvellous fossils. Steve Etches, settled in the village, has built up a collection which even attracts admirers from overseas.

The bay is edged by low, blue-grey shale cliffs, those bands of light-coloured cementstone enlivening its darkness or, at shore level, creating extensive platforms and ledges. At Kimmeridge four major beds take their names from these structures. The Flats, the expanse of stone in the northwest corner of the bay and the point enclosing it, are formed by the thickest, most resilient Flats bed. This is faulted down to sea level several times to create Broad Bench and Long Ebb, thus it divides Kimmeridge Bay from Charnel, Charnel from Hobarrow Bay and Hobarrow Bay from Brandy Bay. A second band, Washing Ledge bed, runs down through the west cliffs of the bay to form Washing Ledge, running out from the shore where the stream joins the sea. At low tide a third, Maple Ledge bed, is revealed as Maple Ledge, connecting the beach with the slipway and cutting the corner where a waterfall descends. The fourth is Yellow Ledge bed, beyond the bay to the east.

Such ledges run gently out to sea, making Kimmeridge a poor place to swim, but at low spring tides rock pools fascinate children and adults come for the diving and wind-surfing. If the bay is not much to look at, it is good to look from. The surroundings are impressive. For us boys it was also the entrance to forbidden lands, a place to lean our bikes against a fence and walk westwards to the shelter of the red flags. As kids we knew this much of its industrial past: oil extracted from the shale had lighted the streets of Paris. We also saw the rusty railway lines above and under the shale cliffs. Only recently have I learned details of those Kimmeridge enterprises, most of which exploited blackstone, bituminous beds in the shale.

The earliest people to bring fire to this shore must have discovered that blackstone burned well. Celia Fiennes comments that 'they take up stones by the shores that are so oyly as the poor burn it for fire it serves for candle too, but it has a strong offensive smell.' Used in hearths for centuries, it leaves a large clinker and its high sulphur content results in that strong smell. It was dropped from common use before WWII.

Iron Age folk also noticed that blackstone took a good polish and, if waxed, could compete with jet as a decorative stone. They set up little workshops across Purbeck, often far from the outcrops, manufacturing a variety of items, especially bracelets. At first these were shaped by hand. The introduction of the hand-lathe around the middle of the first century AD revolutionised the industry. By 300 AD its products were reaching the Scottish

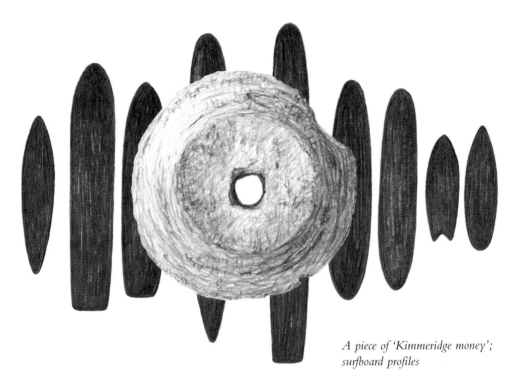

A piece of 'Kimmeridge money';
surfboard profiles

border and northern France. Lathe-turning created 'Kimmeridge Money', discs of shale that confused their finders until the mid 19th century when they were recognised as the cores left from bracelet-making. Fragments of flint and broken bracelet, coupled with the 'Kimmeridge Money', are found at several places across Purbeck. There are sites west of Gaulter Gap and on the clifftop northeast of Rope Lake Head but also at Green Island.

This earliest industry was an unqualified success. Shale must have been exploited in the middle ages, when Abbot of Cerne's writ ran in Kimmeridge, but its sure history starts later and is accompanied by consistent failure. Alum, important in the dyeing process, was produced here in the late 16th century with sufficient success to attract government eyes. Sir William Clavell, who launched a major manufacturing project, was caught in patent problems. Having invested heavily and built a stone jetty inspired by the Cobb at Lyme the business was taken from him and soon failed.

To the right of the road, just before the slipway, a glass-furnace was set up in 1615, probably on the remains of the alum works. The entrepreneur was

Sir Robert Mansel, who had patented the use of fossil fuel in glass manufacture. He abandoned the site when his workers found the local blackstone too inefficient. (Coincidentally, two centuries later his brother's heirs would inherit the estate.) Sir William took over the scheme, signing an agreement with Mansel which confined him to marketing his green glass only in southwest England. His glassmaker, Abraham Bigo, soon built a better furnace, but the temptation of the London market proved too strong for Sir William. He broke the agreement, opening himself to legal action. The furnace was destroyed and, already hard hit by the alum debacle, he was bankrupted, sold Barnston and spent time in the Marshallsea Prison. His stone jetty was destroyed by a catastrophic storm in 1745.

Sir William may have built a dock at Clavell's Hard a kilometre east along the coast, which would explain its name. No one attempted to exploit the shale again until the mid 19th century, the age of industrial entrepreneurs. Eight companies rose and fell on Kimmeridge mineral wealth. Only a small percentage of the shale is sufficiently bituminous to be viable. The main deposit, the blackstone bed, is 85cm thick and appears at the clifftop at Cuddle, above Yellow Ledge, to slope down eastwards, occasionally faulted. It reaches beach-level 200 metres east of Clavell's Hard.

The first enterprise, 'The Bituminous Shale Company', was set up in 1848. A new stone quay was built and a tramway to carry shale there. It was shipped to Weymouth and processed to yield pitch, paraffin wax, grease for lubrication, dyes and naptha. A combination of the sulphurous stench and more patent problems killed the project in six years. Another company took over, adding fertiliser and oil to the list of products before handing over to 'Messrs Wanostrocht & Co' in 1858. Supported by French capital, it opened the mining enterprise with a great fanfare. The French Ambassador, Marshal Pelissier, Duc de Malakoff, stopped in Wareham *en route* to Kimmeridge to inspect the works. He gave an address (translated, since he had no English) at the Red Lion and opened a factory to extract oil from the shale. At first business flourished and the company extended the tramway, but it didn't last. Burton Green, writing soon after the business failed, mentions the tramway 'leading to (the pier) from the mines, but of this latter, as an engineering work, perhaps the less said the better'. That is tantalising. If there had been a disaster the story would survive. Perhaps it was constructed too near the cliff face and soon became dangerous. The few surviving illustrations of shale workings show mines sunk into the ground, or tunnels into the cliff long after they were abandoned. The cliff back, but its profile has not altered drastically since I first saw the one remaining tunnel at Clavell's Hard nearly fifty years ago. Still wide open then, its mouth was surrounded by a beautiful green mixture of moss and tufa. Even now, almost blocked by fallen debris, it survives.

The shale industry, grubby and unromantic, inspired few images. Recently, Dr Mansel showed me the small sketchbook of 'JBB' dated 1880 and entitled 'Reminiscences of Smedmore'. Who was JBB? She (surely it is 'she') seems to have been a talented and regular guest of the younger Mansels. A neighbouring Bond, perhaps? Most of the pictures show the family, but two facing each other depict the young people exploring shale tunnels at Clavell's Hard. In one, rails run from a pair of points to enter two mines. Three figures are 'waiting for candles'. A girl in riding-gear watches Ernest Mansel ineffectually pushing 'BM' in a trolley 'till "Dipper Tom" shows us the real state of things'. Presumably there was a brake. This pair of tunnels is quite separate from the single one shown in the second sketch (page ii). 'Dipper Tom' must have been one of the men working the shale, although at that point no commercial extraction was going on. Did the line follow the blackstone seam along a ledge or a tunnel up to Cuddle where it reaches the top? There are pieces of rusty rail at the foot of the cliff but one or two pieces also lie along a slight shelf on the cliff face.

On the strength of orders for shale oil, Wanostrocht and Co built another stone pier and an iron jetty 90m long. The jetty probably stood beside a shallow rectangular dock cut in the ledges just west of Clavell's Hard. The cliff here is low with an artificial terrace where the blackstone has been dug away halfway up its height. The dock enabling shallow-draft barges to approach the cliff is near a waterfall. East of it three rows of augured holes, one still holding part of a metal upright, must mark that jetty. West of the dock two rows of larger sockets would have held the timbers of another pier. Another socket further west still holds a timber.

If Paris was briefly lit from Kimmeridge, elsewhere drilling was producing better oil more cheaply. The business, closing in 1878 even before the workforce could occupy their new cottages, left a sulphurous smell in the air. Green merely says 'The French company got into difficulties through causes which it will be dangerous to refer to.' Doubtful dealings were still sensitive when he wrote eight years later. Other enterprises followed. All soon succumbed. The last company to work the shale, Kimmeridge Oil and Carbon Co (1883-90), also mined it inland and from the shaft constructed a tramway to the jetty, partly coinciding with the permissive path near the coastguard cottages. Finally, a cement-making industry exploiting lime-rich marls closed in the 1900s. Perhaps there should be marks for persistence!

The slipway area was the focus of all the industries. Both tramways led there. When the tide is low it is possible to trace generations of stone piers and groynes constructed from the 17th century onwards. Above the slipway is the headquarters of the Purbeck Marine Wildlife Reserve.

The blackstone is easily set alight. The cliff at Clavell's Hard, where a camper's fire in the early 1970s ignited the bituminous bed, burned for several years with a flameless fire, not at all dramatic. The cliff smoked, stank of sulphur and slowly reddened. The orange burnt rock is still visible near the clifftop, east of the waterfall. This was the only place between Kimmeridge and Hounstout, beyond Encombe, where one could get up the cliff. Now it is a dangerous scramble. The path, precarious when I descended it in 1997 and now quite gone, led down to the man-made terrace along which rails once ran, then down again to the shore.

Until 1949 the War Department also held land at Smedmore. Naval vessels fired at moving targets on rails. A pair of points jutting into midair from the cliff-top 100 metres west of Clavell's Hard was part of the target railway. In the fifties we kids came across a mass of decayed munitions between the shoreline ledges from Encombe to Kimmeridge. Some remain. Following the beach route was simpler then since it was possible to get up the cliff at the two points where it is easiest to be cut off by the tide, Clavell's Hard and west of Encombe's waterfall. There, Freshwater Steps retains the name but not the steps, washed away shortly before April 1978.

Returning from Kimmeridge recently I was caught here. It was late November and cold but I know the tides: being full moon the spring tide would still be low enough to pass the waterfall. I reached there when it was almost dark to find the tide surprisingly high. Then it struck me. After years of wintering in India, I had calculated tides by BST not GMT. There was no alternative to putting my clothes in the rucksack and wading round. Beyond the waterfall the beach had been scoured away by storms, leaving the water suddenly, unexpectedly deep. Caught unaware, I disappeared briefly beneath it. It was not a good day to cycle home in wet clothes!

The ledges running out to sea create shallow water far from shore, always a hazard for careless pleasure boats and great vessels powerless to overcome severe weather. There have been many disasters. The manor of Kimmeridge retains ancient rights to wreckage on that coast and applied them successfully in 1872 in a dispute between the estate and the Admiralty over possession of a fine timber mast. The keel of a recent victim lies at the top of the beach just east of Clavell's Hard. I passed just after it was washed up in August 1992, its owners salvaging what they could as a couple of coastguards looked on. There were only fragments of white fibreglass, lifejackets, some battered tins of ham - and that solid metal keel. Earlier, just before Christmas, the Firing Range boat had succumbed. It hovers ready to harass any craft that chooses to risk gunfire by cutting straight across from St Aldhelm's Head to Weymouth. During a strong southwest wind it slipped its mooring ready to move away, but the engine failed to start and the crew had to abandon ship, leaving it to smash on the rocks below Hounstout. Of an unknown wreck off Encombe all that remains, draped in weed and visible only at lowest spring tides, is some squared blocks of Portland stone at the end of a ledge, perhaps part of a cargo destined for London.

For loss of life, the worst 20th century tragedy was the wreck of the *Treveal* in 1920, described in detail in David Pushman's recent book. His grandfather, Frank Lander, received a medal for his involvement in the rescue. The vessel grounded firmly on the ledges south of Encombe as a storm grew ever more intense. Sure that she was breaking up, the captain gave orders to abandon ship into a fierce sea. The crew made for Chapmans Pool but only seven of the 43 people on board survived. The ship weathered the storm, its stove still warm next day. The *Treveal* lay there many months until she was blown up.

The undercliff of Hounstout forms a headland of jumbled rocks between Egmont and Chapmans Pool. On it, just above the beach but gradually falling away, is the ruin of Powder House. A solid little building, once with paved floor, it is said to have been a powder magazine. Any cannon set up here disappeared long since. It probably derived from a plan drawn up in 1796 by William Morton Pitt of Encombe and William Clavell of Smedmore to defend Purbeck from the French.

Chapmans Pool is a place of flotsam. Here flotsam and bodies wash in, funnelled into the bay on prevailing southwesterlies. Valuable cargoes turn up, too: drums of oil, mahogony, pine planks. One storm is still famous for its grapefruit. We would find dark green glass 'submarine balls' amongst the driftwood on the tideline. Modern, tougher plastic floats have replaced them. Probably there was no Chapman, the name referring to the spur dividing the valley. East Man and West Man are similar features near Winspit. Was this Short Man which became Chapman? Some old maps mark it Shipman's Pool.

Until 1978 a field above the bay served as a car park, tickets being sold at a kiosk on the road leading to Worth. I came here first in the early fifties in Richard Dunham's father's two-tone car and, swimming, learned that those large mauve and green anemones sting children's tender skin. We descended to the beach past a concrete pillbox but it fell before the advancing sea. Now only fragments remain amongst the shingle.

In the summer of 1961 a tame Atlantic Grey Seal held court at Chapmans Pool, hero of Nina Warner Hook's book, 'Seal Summer'. It would sit out on the slipway and seeing visitors, it lumbered into the sea, swam across and chugged up the beach, catching a hand gently in its dog-like mouth. Some people brought fish, which it ate more from politeness than desire.

Erosion and fear of litigation closed the road. The cliffs moved on the melt-water from the 1978 blizzard. '28th Feb: set off up the side of Pier Bottom and along the top of Emmett towards Chapmans Pool. Could see a fair amount of movement beneath me but soon before I reached the badger track there was a massive rock fall down into the trees below...made my way down to Chapmans Pool crossing the remnants of the road that Reg Prior and Dicky

Bartlett were trying to establish down to the slipway. A large part of it has been entirely obliterated. The stream must be having difficulty cutting back the mud as it collapses into it.'

Dicky Bartlett went down as the land slipped, leaving hurriedly when movement caused barbed wire fencing to twang and break. In a sad era where culprits must be sought, financial compensation must be extracted, the Encombe estate felt unable to bear the risk. Chapmans Pool was officially closed and all but those intrusive roaring white speedboats have to make an effort to get there.

In the wake of several bad wrecks a lifeboat service was set up here in 1867. (Kimmeridge also had one from 1871 to 1896.) The boat was housed in a stone-tiled boathouse at the head of the slipway. The building remains but the tile fell in the 1970s. There was rarely any call for that lifeboat so it was withdrawn at the end of that century. Coastguard cottages beside the track along the south side of the valley were demolished, but in summer a burst of cultivated roses still appears by the store. Foundations and a single storeroom remain. In 1976 Col. Scott of Encombe granted its use to Trevor Squires and other bird-ringers. Trevor, supported by Alan Lander, started ringing at Chapmans Pool in 1971. These ringers have helped to discover that most British Chiffchaffs winter in the same area of Senegal, each favouring one particular bush.

Chapmans Pool slipway was the haven for fishermen living in Worth and Kingston. Everyday through the summer months they set out in their boats to haul and rebait pots. The crab and lobster season runs from March to October, crabs, they say, being at their best when there is an 'r' in the month. For bait they turned not only to unwanted fish and their offal but also to dead livestock, including horses. The prawn season runs from August to December and the technique is different. Smaller pots are used, or circular dip nets. The nets are put down in late evening or night. Bait is strung across the circular frame attached by rope to a float. A series of nets are set then hauled when the prawns have had time to gather.

Before the Second World War pots were hand-made from withies cut in the bed at Worth. Nets were set in the Pool or across the long channel between some of the Kimmeridge ledges. When there was no wind to fill their sails, most fishermen relied on their oars. The Landers of Worth, who have fished out of Chapmans Pool since the latter 19th century, got their first motorised boat in the 1930s. It was powered by a 10 horse power car engine. During the war this coast was closed for fishing. When it resumed other fishermen bought engines and ready-made wire pots took over from woven willow. The only pots of my boyhood were woven and most villages had a withy bed in a damp corner. That at Worth still survives. The willows, no longer pollarded, have grown to become a stand of trees below the pond.

Wire gave way to modern plastic-coated steel-framed pots and the nets, once hemp, are now polypropylene. Perhaps romantic Iron men looked wistfully back to Bronze, yet one material surplants another because it is better suited to a task.

Even in the Pool the sea could be treacherous. Landlord of the Square and Compass, Charlie Newman's grandfather, also Charlie, drowned here in 1948. He had gone out in rough conditions to pull his net when his boat overturned. Although he could swim he didn't make it to the shore. In winter most fishermen turned to quarrying for employment. The Landers are the only professional fishermen working there today. Their present fibreglass boat has advanced a long way from the old clinker-built boats. Charlie Lander no longer has to lug his catch up Fisherman's Walk which, truncated by landslips at its seaward end, runs diagonally up the hillside. He can drive to the slipway, although the track shifts most winters. In 2004 he was victim of a series of attacks by 'the Lobster Liberation Front'. Coming at night to this isolated spot these sad folk smashed his pots, then returned to sabotage his boat. It is so easy to destroy a man's livelihood, his 'heritage'.

Encombe Estate Accounts for 1929 list four men (including Frank and Miller Lander) paying an annual £1 rent for huts at Chapmans Pool. Others paid a shilling for a 'boat haul' - the right to park a boat and use the slipway. Trev had his first boat there in 1964, an elderly black and white clinker-built dinghy. We both used it for exploring the coast and for fishing. Energetic with the baler, I continued several years after he'd condemned it. That boat ended up as a film extra.

In those summer days there were often dead tope or conger around the slipway, caught by Barry Candy and left, presumably for the Landers to use as bait. Later, I had my own marine ply pram dinghy there and now share with Pete a little fibreglass tender. It is ideal for running over the ledges, looking down into the clear water, weed swaying in the tide and fish cruising through it. In the early summer slow-moving spider crabs, come to spawn, are easily snatched in the shallows and there are mackerel and pollack to be caught on lures. Always rowing, not farting more petrol fumes into a damaged world.

Up the valley from Chapmans Pool along the west side of Short Man, if it be such, is Kingston village. West Hill, flanking it, forms one wall of Encombe's gentle valley.

KINGSTON AND ENCOMBE

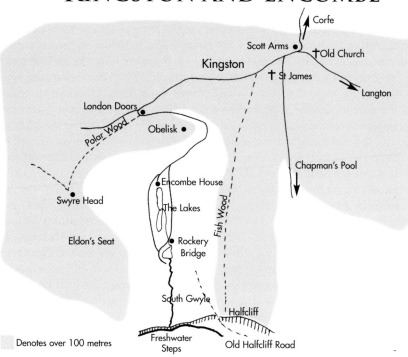

To us boys Kingston was different from Purbeck's other villages. It was heavily overshadowed by Lord Eldon and his heirs, by the oversized church dedicated to their, not God's greater glory. It had an all-pervading air of feudalism, being too small, too close to escape the shadow of Encombe House. Even Sir Ernest Scott, known as a benevolent, unpretentious squire (Mary tells of him happily cycling up through Langton in prewar days, on his way back from Swanage), was for all that one of the greatest landlords in Purbeck. The folk of Kingston were his tenants. It was wise to remember.

There was already a meek church when the first Earl took over, a mediaeval building to the east of the village. He gave it a total makeover in 1833 but it remained modest and traces of its Norman origin survive, including the dog-tooth arch embedded over the west door. Here he was buried in 1838. It continued as parish church until 1922 but that was a nominal role. The Cavendish-Bentinck clan still retain a vault in its churchyard where some at

30

least of the Dukes of Portland lie. The formal shift to the cathedral-like private chapel was merely recognition of a *fait accomplit*. The new building took over Sunday services from its completion in 1880, leaving to the old church village funerals and weddings. Then it stood empty, sometimes used as a village hall, until it was sold in 1977 and became a house.

The building of the towering church was the greatest event to touch Kingston in the 19th century. The third Earl, then aged 28 did not skimp on it. As architect he needed the best, so he called in a distant relative of mine, Sir George Street. (His direct descendant, also George Street, fascinated us kids. Severely deaf, he would appear with some similarly-handicapped friend with whom he chatted happily in sign language. Not only that, he could lip read. We had to be on our guard!) Street was a master of the neo-Gothic, most famous for the fairy tale fantasy (nightmare to some) of the Law Courts in the Strand in London.

Victorian craftsmanship could be spectacular. The Industrial Revolution and Imperial trade provided wealth for patronage, hand tools were at their best and there was no dearth of material or skill in Purbeck. This was to be a vernacular version of the Early English style. For stone he turned largely to two Upper Purbeck beds proved by mediaeval builders and Portland freestone, all outcropping on Eldon's land. He chose freestone for the interior walls and Purbeck marble for contrasting pillars and shafts. For the outer fabric he picked burr, a stone favoured by both Saxon and Norman builders. It is resilient, despite the vulnerable patches developing into hollows in its surface. A century has masked the natural grey-brown with pink algae.

Between 1874 and 1880 the construction of St James's kept many local masons busy. Later, they complained that it caused them to neglect a loyal clientele. It proved hard to rekindle a market when the church was complete. But it stands to their memory, a masterpiece of meticulous 19th century craftsmanship. A neat little watercolour in the Smedmore sketchbook shows three figures, a top-hatted man with two girls climbing the grassy scarp towards Kingston on their way to a Sunday afternoon service. It was 1880 and the great church was a novelty. Duty would have compelled them to appear at Kimmeridge of a Sunday morning so it is doubtful if they continued to attend.

Sited to form a prominent landmark over much of Purbeck, the church has an aspect almost as sinister as that of the mediaeval castle it overlooks. There was also a contemporary mock-Tudor Parsonage to go with it. The whole concept of 'squarson', a parson drawn from the ranks of the squirarchy stands in unpleasant contrast to the priesthood elsewhere in Europe. Victorian wealth rose on the back of Dickensian poverty quite as certainly as western prosperity calls for third world subservience. John Betjeman may have liked St James's. I don't. Nor do I like the modern floodlighting that elevates it still further. The destruction of night is a tragedy overlooked by those who fail to venture out after sunset. Reality persists after light fades and darkness is nothing to fear. It harbours the inspiring mystery of the night sky, spattered with stars retreating forever. It can be tamed by a simple torch without inflicting a half-light on the rural world.

Apart from fine masonry work the church has two things to its credit: its bells and its view. On a still evening at Dunshay the bells are just audible, and I appreciate them. As for the view, one of my class-mates, Vernon Henstridge (Vermin, we called him), was son of the dairyman at Encombe. Not only did he give me legitimate access to the valley, he knew the local lore. That included where they hid the key to the tower. I remember the first ascent, the empty tower long neglected. We crunched up through the darkness on an inch of anciently-dead flies which carpeted each tread of the stone steps. Gaining the blinding light of the summit, we surreptitiously overlooked so much of Purbeck. In those days there was but one view to beat it, that from the great steel pylon west of Worth and I only saw it once.

The local pub bore the peerage name, the Eldon Arms, until soon after 1926 when the popular third Earl died. Because the fourth Earl had married a Catholic, his father left the estate to his second son, Sir Ernest Scott. In 1953 it passed to his nephew, Col Harold Scott. For us the regime in the valley was always that of 'the Colonel'. Then the pub became the Scott Arms. When we were youths it was one of four dim, cosy country pubs we frequented: the Scott, the Square, the Kings Arms and the Fox. Posed patiently in a glass case in the main room was a stuffed hen harrier. It expanded to cater for an outside clientele, folk who liked red plush, false panelling and copper bed-pans. Certainly, it has a wonderful view down to Corfe but I rarely go there and it can do without me!

It is hard to think of Kingston as an historic village because of a makeover in the 1770s, no less thorough than that to church or pub. All the cottages were rebuilt by a philanthropic squire, Morton Pitt. He also founded a small rope-making industry to benefit the villagers. Generous but unbusinesslike, eventually in 1807 he was compelled to sell Encombe to the Lord Chancellor. So little of Kingston is old but its name, derived from centuries of royal ownership from Saxon times when it was indeed a king's town. In the last fifty years much of the life of the village has gone. The school-house, built in memory of the 2nd Lord Eldon in 1856, was closed in 1958 when the few remaining pupils were moved to Corfe.

In 2003 Encombe House, the valley and Chapmans Pool were sold to Charles McVeigh. The Scotts retain the village and much of the estate.

There are several interpretations for 'Encombe'. Some say that is means 'great valley', others that a version used in 1224, Hennecumbe, points to it being a 'valley of birds', especially water hens. Hutchins, never at a loss, suggests 'end of the valley'.

The Kingston estate passed from Shaftesbury Abbey to the Crown at the Dissolution, then through two owners in quick succession. Both upset Henry VIII and lost their heads. Robert Culliford bought it in the 17th century and built the first Encombe House. His son, William, a reliable member of The Board of Customs, compiled an important report in 1681 on corruption in the service. Kingston was sold to William Pitt in 1694 and in 1734 his son, George Pitt, bought Encombe. The next in line, John, remodelled the Culliford house using Purbeck Portland stone for the new exterior. It remains the core of the present building. A small village shown in some 18th century paintings was demolished when the valley was landscaped to create a suitable environment for the house. Presumably the unpicturesque villagers were rehoused in Kingston.

Encombe passed to William Morton Pitt, a liberal MP for 36 years and cousin to the prime minister, William Pitt the Younger. Morton Pitt became an important figure in the Purbeck of his time. More philanthropic than prudent, he ran through a fortune and was eventually compelled to sell off his Purbeck holdings. Lord Eldon, arch-reactionary Lord Chancellor, having acquired nearby Scoles in 1792, bought Encombe from Pitt in 1807. Did he relish the submission of such a stern political opponent? Elizabeth Ham, staying at Norden in 1820 recounts how, when Eldon was at Encombe, documents came down from London to have the Great Seal affixed. 'One day there was a great fire in one of the rooms, and Lord Eldon hid the Great Seal in the hollow root of a tree. This was the time of the Queen's trial...'

One of two gifted brothers of modest Newcastle coal-dealing stock, Lord Eldon fought every piece of progressive legislation that came his way. He opposed Catholic Emancipation and the Great Reform Bill of 1832 before retiring to Encombe. His end was sad. Not only was he uneasy with retirement but all his closest kin predeceased him. His children, including his heir, died, then his wife. Only his favourite dog, Pincher, outlived him. His heirs gradually spent less time here and by 1909 the house was closed and shuttered.

Beside Encombe House are a walled garden and a palladian temple inside which, overlooking the swimming pool a greening bronze youth, a gladiator, stood. One late June evening ten years back, we took a digger along the private road via Hill Bottom and down into the valley, Trev driving whilst I unlocked the gates. The mission was to raise the confused bronze youth, then perched on rollers outside his temple, back onto his plinth, which had been re-erected in the open air. The Scotts and their agent sat by the pool, an evening drink rudely interrupted by our arrival. The new focus of the shrine was a white refrigerator from which cold drinks came forth, but not as far as us. Looking around at the beauty of the valley in high summer, the lakes and the handsome low grey house, then at the table beside the pool, did I envy its ownership? It seemed a prison. Since then, even the gladiator has made a break for freedom, escaping the valley to more-modest Orchard Hill Farm. But life there has its hazards. Recently, some boy scouts from a nearby camp were caught pushing moss up the poor fellow's bottom.

The 18th century stables are let as flats. Down the valley stand two more houses, the last of which was the dairyman's, dim and stone-flagged, where Vernon lived. On the hilltop overlooking the descending road stands a tall cliffstone obelisk erected in 1835 by the first Earl to his brother, Baron Stowell, who was to die the following year. Local people spotted it in the background of the 1960s film of *Far From the Madding Crowd*, which was largely shot around Purbeck. It fell during a gale in winter 1989/90, leaving a deep trench. Some sections rolled right down the hillside. Since it was re-erected there is a sense that it is no longer quite vertical.

From left to right:
a second-century Roman bronze sestertius,
a Victorian farthing, a durtriges Stater, a George VI
penny; a Bee Orchid

In the woodland beyond the house is Rockery Bridge, made from boulders of shelly spangle. It has a grotto indented into it and is crossed by a second road down the valley. It is supposed to be the work of the second Earl, fashionably in search of the picturesque. Trev remarks that a painting shows it with men nearby clad in tricorn hats and spangle would have to be shifted to get at the freestone for work on the house. That suggests the mid 18th century. There is a redundant ice house too, a pre-refrigeration feature of many country houses. A well-lagged, subterranean building usually opening only in the roof, it was filled with ice at any opportunity during the winter. Ice stored in mass would keep through the summer, to be used in preserving food and cooling drinks.

Of the two lakes, the first, elongated, runs back from the lawn in front of the house before draining into the second. In April 1961 '...we went down the valley to the rookery. Here we sat on the lower branches arguing as to whether or not we should ask the Colonel to let us go boating on the lake...We walked up to the entrance of the Big House where I waited for Vernon to ask. He soon returned...we descended into the boathouse and got out the big and heavy boat. We wanted to go on the south part of the lake and to the island and therefore had to cross a causeway about 6 inches above water level. The boat was heavy and ...managed to swing round using the causeway as a pivot and push Vernon into the water.'

A stream drains the lakes to flow down South Gwyle past low ash trees which, easily climbed, held that rookery. Beyond, it plunges over the cliff at Freshwater Steps where, instead of cutting into the cliff-top, the waterfall projects out from it on a little headland. This odd feature owes its existence to the stream, which keeps the shale constantly wet. Elsewhere, the dry cliff-face crumbles, giving rise to continual little landslides onto the pebble beach, each leaving a puff of dust. In the fifties the waterfall ran handsomely over the end of the point but over the years it has shifted, taking a shortcut to fall over the west side and threatening to truncate the promontory. Walking to Encombe from Chapmans Pool at low tide, I would come this way, climbing Freshwater Steps from the beach. They have gone, leaving only stone with iron stubs set in lead and fragments of concrete. For a time there was a rope ladder, a simple rope, then nothing. Encombe folk have had no access to the sea ever since.

Beside the road a stone-lined ditch runs from the top of the valley towards the house. It rarely contains water. The source of most of the valley's fresh water, thus the stream itself, is a masterpiece of Victorian engineering. The second Earl, faced with a water shortage had a stone-lined tunnel cut through West Hill. It is 1/2 mile long with a gradient of 1 in 866, masonry-lined with three vertical ventilation shafts. The water comes from a spring on the near side of the neighbouring valley and another beyond it in Hill

Bottom, both near the 100m contour line. Almost 4km of cast iron pipes carry water from the springs to a reservoir near the house. It is channelled into Encombe's pump-house and from there some 320,000 litres of water a day flows to reservoirs across the estate. It passes onwards through 32 km of pipes to supply the valley and Kingston village as well as ten farms on the estate.

A ruined pump house just above the waterfall used to draw salt water up from a round opening east of the waterfall promontory, supplying it to the house. That intake is occasionally visible at low spring tide when the sea has scoured out the sand that buries it. This was another of the second Earl's innovations, salt water then being fashionable for healthy bathing.

A route into the valley, made by the second Earl is almost lost to memory. Descending the road from Kingston towards Chapmans Pool he would divert slightly, passing below Westhill Wood. Look carefully and you can still see the shadow of a track across the meadow to a point at the foot of the stepped section of the coastal path. There it passed through a still-clear cutting onto the undercliff. That route, through Halfcliff, not only descended more gently than its alternatives but also approached the house more elegantly past the lake to arrive at its handsome façade. The shale has slipped away, taking the road with it, but when we were boys it was still possible to follow it through the undergrowth to come out through a similar nick in the cliff-top onto the hillside above Encombe Valley. There were walls along the way, introduced trees and shrubs and terracotta pipes drained the surfaced track. The undercliff must once have been cultivated. An apple tree still clings on. Vernon used to come this way with his collie, Flossie, to meet us at Chapmans Pool. During every prolonged period of rain the undercliff slips further. Ever more thickly overgrown, the old way is abandoned to brambles. Below it, in summer, there is often a flush of bee orchids.

Today, the main, private road to Encombe passes west through Kingston then onwards for almost a mile, past botanically-interesting woodland before turning down into the valley at London Doors. No doors remain, only an ugly pair of stone gateposts, the ashlar deeply-chamfered to accentuate each joint. That way the Earl left Londonwards. Several unmetalled tracks into the woods (one bearing the footpath to Hounstout) join to form an alternative road that passes an abandoned quarry, source of Purbeck Portland stone used on the estate, to run into the main road. As a boy I took none of these, turning off the Hounstout track to descend helter-skelter down Dark Walk, a steep woodland path rank with wild garlic in the spring, short-cutting the formal curvaceous descent to join the road at the bottom.

I remember tearing down there on an August day in 1960. Vernon had telephoned, describing a strange bird feeding in one of the fields. Only one species fitted and that set me pedalling straight up to Kingston. There, feeding amongst the herring gulls, was a glorious red-breasted goose. Anyone cold to all forms of bird but provided with minimal aesthetic sense would respond to that one. Its startling design of black and chestnut divided by prominent white outlines inspired the ancient Egyptians to depict it faithfully within their tombs. Belonging to Siberia, it bore no ring on its leg to indicate any other origin, but the chance of its being a wild bird blown off course were very small. What did I care? It was beautiful.

Encombe is a lovely, private valley, walled on three sides by steep descents and uncrossed by footpaths save at the cliff. It is overlooked, however, by footpaths running around its rim. The track to Swyre Head past Polar Wood gives a fair bird's eye view of the Golden Bowl, as they call the valley. An odd, smoothly-rounded dome of a hillock rises from its northern floor where the soft shales have been protected from erosion by a cap of glacial gravel. On the east flank of the valley is Fish Wood, a vast piece of topiary, its trees set out in the form of a fish swimming towards the sea. The shape remains clear but its head is damaged.

We grew up with a tale of a wartime plane crashing into Polar Wood. History didn't relate whether it was German or British, perhaps because Bob Dorey, in his memoir of a century in Kingston, places it before the war, with four men killed just above the house. Our story continued that Mrs Scott's hair turned white overnight after seeing those mangled men. Why check such tales? They reflect the spirit, if not the truth.

'Swyre' means a neck of land or a col. Swyre Head forms the valley's west wall, its highest point crowned by an artificial hillock. Until recently I believed implicitly that Swyre was created a little lower than Creech Barrow, on the rival Bond estate and that Lord Eldon had built the hillock so that he should own the highest point in Purbeck. Certainly, the barrow seems to have been built up not long ago. Modern maps show Swyre's height as 203m against Creech's 193 m and the bump is less than 3m high. Perhaps his lordship added a little, including the stone block on its summit, to enhance his superiority but the barrow is Bronze Age. The view to the west is formidable, taking in the coast to Kimmeridge and beyond, along ragged Gad, the white gashes of Cockpit Head and Whitenothe, to faint Weymouth and Portland Bill.

One late summer many years ago a group of us tripped on 'acid' at Swyre. To the west the wheat was not long cut and, then normal practice, the stubble had been burned to produce a fantastic pattern of golden and black lines. The design was even more wonderful once the deluded mind set it all in motion. Then, running down the hillside we came upon a sheep on its back. That is lethal to a plump, well-fleeced animal. Struggle as it may it is unable to right itself. Pushing the great fluffy thing over onto its feet and seeing it run off was an added surrealistic touch.

Another strange summer day drew a crowd to Swyre to witness the near-total solar eclipse of 11th August 1999. It was odd weatherwise, breeze-blown low cloud thinning and thickening as it crossed the sky. People bore all manner of gadgets to safely view the sun, all requiring a certain degree of focussing, directing. In the event, the sun appeared briefly, faintly, in glimpses that punctuated its darkening and resurgence. A shadow crossed the sea and at the depth of dimness the automatically-triggered street-lights of Poole turned on. Its waterfront sparkled with the tiny flashes of many distant cameras.

That eclipse experience contrasted sharply with another in Rajasthan in 1995. Rabu and I had left home in Churu that morning to travel southwards, despite the pleas of the women of the house. Our route would cross the band of totality as it struck. We were risking life and limb, so they said, by exposing ourselves to its evil effects. As is well-know, eclipses are caused by a demon devouring the sun only to be compelled to regurgitate it by the force of many deities and the prayers of mankind. In deference to modern scientific fashion the danger is explained in terms of excessive radiation. As the sky dimmed we planned to view the totality from a handsome derelict rainwater reservoir a few miles ahead. Rabu, sitting pillion, used a black negative to report the sun's gradual demise. As the false twilight fell National Highway 11 emptied of traffic until, quite alone, we left the road to park in the sand beside the waterless reservoir. There, a blue, deserted dusk fell then faded, a wavering light playing on the white stucco of its walls. The sun returned and, after a decent interval, great laden trucks and tiny white Maruti cars continued their busy transit between Agra and Bikaner.

It is an odd structure, Swyre, a descending neck rising slightly to a second peak before running down towards Eldon's Seat, a favourite refuge of the first Earl, his vigour gone, become an old man. His eldest daughter had the masonry throne set up, a viewpoint over his estate and the coast beyond. One of Leonora Bond's late 19th century watercolours shows it half dismantled. In massive Roman letters 'ELDON SEAT 1835' is deeply inscribed, but in her picture the block bearing 'ELDON' lies inverted. Had the seat proved a little unstable and required rebedding? Beside it is Pincher's headstone.

Looking southeast from his throne the Earl would have seen the rugged cliffs of St Aldhelm's Head, a newly-built row of coastguard cottages at their summit.

ROUND THE HEAD

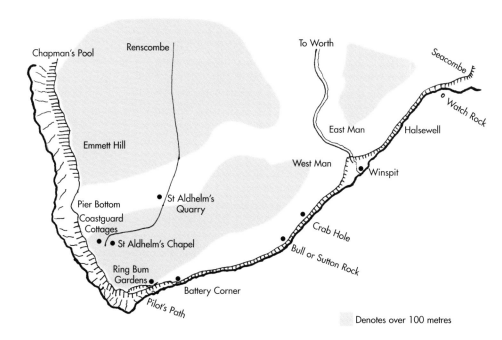

South from Chapmans Pool the rugged cliff of Emmett Hill runs above a grassy slope of soft shale. Did 'emmett', an ant, refer to an anthill tumulus, now half fallen, perched on that clifftop? Or does it, as some aver, define a windward-facing bluff. Undermined by soft shale great blocks of stone have fallen, creating a jungle undercliff and a rocky shore. We first struggled pointlessly the length of that undercliff when men from the RAF camp still walked above, adding to the hazards by innocently hurling rocks down. The trees grew until a pair of buzzards settled amongst them. At dusk sharp, shy foxes and close badgers nosing their way break the cliff's silhouette to forage in the fields and Worth's weekend dustbins. When living nearby I would watch the traffic, the badgers pawing bundled hay backwards towards their sett. Returning from fishing I would gift them a mackerel.

Andrei, a White Russian from Hongkong, lived down there in the early 1970s. A young architecture student cast in the hippie mould, he was brightly drifting out of reality. His 'far-out' plans included flying a balloon to the sun by celestial music. He had a lurcher, Rosie, and two cats, all black and white. We had shared a cottage in Worth until he went away one weekend (it lasted a fortnight), leaving me with one cat. It promptly gave birth on my trousers. Honourable, he gave me another, better pair before moving to the undercliff with his dependents.

He had cut out the hardboard segments of a geodesic dome with a snugly-fitting round door, which he set up on a platform of driftwood. It never bore its crown of transparent perspex. The site he picked had at its centre a single slender young rowan which must go if the roof were to be closed. That was out of the question, so when it rained, it rained on man and beast alike. He drew water from a nearby spring. Eventually, his home was smashed during one of his absences. Recently, Pete and I looked for the place with only that rowan to guide us. Just one was visible, but it was old and gnarled. Time passes. It was the same tree. In the undergrowth lay those perspex sections, never integrated into the fabric but surviving all.

A steep-sided dry valley, Pier Bottom, divides Emmett Hill from the tip of St Aldhelm's Head. It was cut when Ice Age permafrost prevented the surface water from seeping away. In the evening, the sun low, there are clear shadow traces of early folk - boundaries of Celtic fields, a redundant diagonal track on the valley side. The headland was busy in Iron Age times. In March 1982 Mr Bugler, ploughing just east of the quarry, uncovered a cylindrical chamber almost four metres deep. Roger Peers, then curator at Dorchester Museum, identified it as a prehistoric grain store. The farmer, David Strange allowed a team from Southampton University to spend several seasons after harvest uncovering a small settlement. Such sites are not uncommen in Purbeck, but proximity to our everyday life set this one apart.

Another track, a low terrace above the valley floor, was lightly metalled and must have carried stone from nearby quarries towards the pier. That pier, setting its face into the prevailing wind, gave the valley its name. It was probably built during the 18th century, using great, shaped blocks of cliffstone, Portland stone so-called because it forms the cliffs between here and Durlston Head. It may have barely projected but stood as a hard beside an inlet cleared through rocks, deep enough for a boat to come alongside at high tide. Someone had invested heavily to export stone. Mass quarrying of 'Purbeck Portland' began in the mid 18th century with the huge Ramsgate harbour project. An inexhaustible supply of material, given calm weather, could be loaded onto merchant vessels and delivered straight to the site. Cliffstone was used much earlier but it was a minor resource before Ramsgate. The pier must have been built to handle stone for it. Between June 1750 and September 1752 15,000 tons were sent there, between January 1764 and January 1771 a further 94,000 tons. The project's trustees set aside fifty sailing vessels to transport it.

Everything about this pier is hypothetical. It appears on no map, no picture records it and its existence seems to earn no mention in documents. Perhaps it succumbed to a great storm too soon to leave much mark. Was the storm of 1745 too early? Was the Great Gale of 1824, breaching the Fleet and the Cobb at Lyme, too late? Some fifty squared blocks remain on the shore, some cut with notches to hold half of a double dovetail of wood or stone to weld neighbouring blocks together. One piece held an iron ring set in lead.

Above the pier at the mouth of the valley a large cannon stood upended amongst rusty barbed wire entanglements, juxtaposing two eras of coastal defence. Does that indicate that the pier still stood until the Napoleonic Wars? Similar to one at Hedbury, it disappeared for scrap around 1960.

There are several indentations high on the sides of Pier Bottom, perhaps dug to test the stone. One, at the head of the valley, is marked as a 'Stone Pitt' on an early 18th century map and that is the only quarry still producing worked Purbeck Portland stone. St Aldhelm's Quarry was reopened in the 1930s by Mr Davy, once manager of Seacombe Quarry. Unable to clear debts, he handed over the quarrying rights to Mr Haysom. The family has worked it ever since.

Overlooking the cliff at St Aldhelm's Head a hammer-shaped pair of rocks are all that remain of the cliff's pre-quarrying profile. Purbeck's cliffs display a landscape free of planners. All the favourite spots - Winspit, Seacombe, Dancing Ledge, Tilly Whim Caves - are abandoned quarries. Planners require a false, 'restored' landscape. The chasm of Swanworth Quarry offered enormous possibilities as a micro-environment but huge sums are spent pretending it never happened. During the 1980s owners of inland quarries were required to conceal them behind earthworks. Meanwhile, tourism focuses on the unhomogenised. Where underground quarries survive from the pre-planner world they are busily preserved and labelled as heritage sites. Heritage doesn't stop. Will our offering be pathetic, apologetic attempts to cover up traces of our passing?

Sometimes we boys cadged a lift on the little grey Dodge lorry taking the men to work at St Aldhelm's Quarry. Burt Norman, who drove it, was a cheerful, good-natured man, the sort to stop if he overtook us busily cycling his way. There, I first met Geoff Hooper. I was shy of those men but Geoff, always cheerful and built like 'a brick shit-house', related well to us boys. Having left school at fourteen, National Service took him to post-war Germany where he exploited a retentive memory and an inquiring mind. He acquired a wide education as well as fluency in German, reading Goethe, Heine and Rilke in the original. His poetry brought an offer of a fellowship at an American university. By the 1950s he was working in the quarries, first out at St Aldhelm's Head then, till he died aged 74, with Kevin Keates. All the while he built up his collection of poems.

I worked at St Aldhelm's Quarry intermittently for thirty years, subsidising travel and research in India by sawing and polishing stone. In the fifties much of the sound was clinking hammer on punch, wooden mallet on chisel. Now almost everything is mechanised. The quarry face comprises the topmost Portland beds of which we used, from the top, blue-grey shelly Blue Bit, then more shelly light brown Spangle which grades down into Pond Freestone, a fine, shell-free limestone excellent for masonry work. Both the Duke and Duchess of Windsor lie beneath Pond Freestone ledgers from St Aldhelm's Quarry. The stone here is finer than at Portland but more fragmented. Purbeck stone block was brought in from around Acton to be stored ready for processing.

Stone must be dug early, so that it dries before the first heavy frost, which can cause destructive cracks in wet block. We released each block, working at lines of weakness with steel wedges and bars. Some we cut, drilling a line of holes six inches apart, into each putting a pair of 'feathers' - eared strips of steel - with a 'plug' (steel wedge) between. A biddle (sledge-hammer) was played along the plugs, xylophone-like, giving each several blows. The 'chink' of steel against steel rises in pitch with the pressure until the crisp sound of fracture. The sections were then worked apart. Today, a large digger rapidly tears out the season's block.

To shift block from the face to the workshop there was a pair of wooden cranes, the last in a Dorset quarry. One was a veteran of Dancing Ledge. These rotated through a large arc. A chain was put round the block. Otherwise, it was 'dogged' - a shallow hole punched in either end a few inches below the top - to be lifted with a pair of heavy steel 'nips' - opposing hooks running freely on a looped chain attached to the crane's hook. The point of each 'nip' was held in a 'dog' hole as the crane took the strain. The pressure on the triangle of chain kept them in place. Two men worked the crane, slipping a cog across into high gear as they took the weight. The block was lowered onto a bogey and pushed along rails under the workshop gantry crane, to be lifted onto the steel table of a circular saw or set up on the bogey of a frame saw. A variable number of diamond-toothed blades are fitted at measured intervals into the swinging frame, which an electric motor moves to and fro as an adjustable ratchet slowly lowers it. Water cools the blades and keeps the cuts free of slurry and the saw stops automatically when the stone is cut through. Soft Pond Freestone cuts at about 30cm an hour. The resulting unshaped slabs, generally cut along the bed, are stacked for later use. They are sawn to shape then, if required, polished with a machine oddly christened a 'Jenny Lind' after the Swedish opera singer. For masonry work there is a planer and a lathe. Today, a computerised saw can cut complex

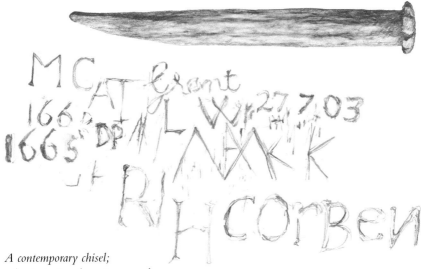

A contemporary chisel;
a bent nineteenth-century punch;
various graffiti inside St. Aldhelm's Chapel

mouldings quicker and more accurately than a craftsman. The lament of Purbeck's stone industry is that the block is too small and too full of flaws.

The quarry's busy rabbit population suffered from resurgences of myxamatosis and from stoats, a sharp scream signalling another slain. When its teeth clutch a victim a stoat is oblivious of its surroundings and we could approach within a yard. We cherished a number of adders, which sunned themselves on a grassy bank until an alien hand, thinking to do us a favour, killed them all.

Living in a caravan there, I was in Worth when the blizzard of Saturday 18th February 1978 struck. Next morning I walked '...back to the quarr despite continuing snow and gales. The most difficult place was getting into the first field near the coastguards'... wallowed a bit in a drift near Scripture Gate then crossed the road to St Aldhelm's Head into the field on the west side (the road itself was drifted solid)...All day the wind and snow continued, the sky a sort of slate blue and the snow blowing over the road into the quarry. The shed had become a shelter for birds - greenfinches, linnets and chaffinches – struggled across to reach it. A Lapwing landed briefly, then flew off. Around the caravan a wall of snow was growing, beautifully sculpted.' . By Monday: 'The snow had stopped ...walked into the shed and noticed that the roof above the frame saw was going – cracking away as the beams snapped – the mason's shed roof was buckling under the weight of snow. I'd intended to stay indoors all day to nurse a cold but this was too desperate. Found a shovel near the frame – a silent prayer as I passed under the cracking roof – climbed on the gantry crane and dug away a patch on the mason's shed roof sufficient to stand on then got up and started to clear the roof. Had got halfway with the job when Brian Bugler appeared carrying a shovel. He got a ladder and started on the roof above the frame, which continued to crack. I joined him when I'd finished – the snow was well above his head over the flywheel...'

★

At the tip of St Aldhelm's Head ragged stone makes an extensive undercliff which falls abruptly to a rock-strewn shore. Here men worked the fallen block into gatepost globes, sinks, ashlar and, most commonly, mushroom-like staddle stones to support grain-stores, keeping rats at bay. Broken fragments remain. These were manoeuvred onto boats near where: 'on March 8th or 9th a 500 ton boat – the *Sand Dart* – ran aground on the rocks during thick fog and to date, despite attempts and battering waves, has stayed firmly lodged (April 15th 1962). I visited the wreck on March 10th and tried to learn my Shylock part while watching her.' The ship, a sand dredger, suffered a wreck without drama, always open to rumour as to how it might possibly have happened. The ship was moving fast enough, the tide high enough to glide it firmly onto the rocks and keep it there. The crew climbed overboard and, making their way up the cliff, walked to Worth. Frank Honour, the mate, never got much further. Finding the Square and Compass congenial he settled there, working for Eileen Newman, then landlady, and doing other jobs around the area until he died.

Vain attempts were made to tow the Sand Dart off, but it was stuck until the extreme tides of September. Neither of us had a boat then, so we eyed the clinker-built lifeboat that lay unsalvaged on deck. Just when the temptation became too much someone lit a fire, burning a narrow, terminal strip up its side. Having salvaged the valuable items the owners left the rest. I had its red cargo book, which listed trips to and fro between Plymouth, Portsmouth, Shoreham and other south coast ports. The distress flares were the star event at a party on Nine Barrow Down but kept Poole lifeboat out all night. It never occurred to us that, from Poole, those red flares would appear to come from behind Brownsea Island. One memento of the *Sand Dart* is a rusty steel cable (although Trev reckons it was there earlier) still leading across the scree towards the shore.

High above, at the end of the Head, the long-derelict 12th century chapel has become a fashionable venue for weddings. Lord Eldon had it repaired and reconsecrated in 1874, a cross added, but even afterwards it was used as a coastguard store. An 1880s watercolour by the Reverend Moule shows crossed grapples set on the wall and a box labelled 'rocket line'. Nothing is known of the chapel's earlier history. Oddly oriented, its corners facing the cardinal points, it stands in the middle of prehistoric earthworks. Was the chapel intended to counteract or benefit from their magic?

Some say there was a beacon on the chapel to guide ships at night: an agile monk to light it and resilient stone to bear the heat! It may have born something as a navigation point. Posed on solid Portland beds, most of its fabric is burr, outcropping on the valley-side 5 km away, and there are pieces of Ham Stone from distant Ilminster. Odd, in a period when transport was hard.

We grew up knowing of its association with magic, knowing that folk used to drop votive offerings into the hollows so characteristic of burr in the hope of a wish fulfilled. For centuries the place must have been isolated from the nearest dwelling, visited only intentionally not by passers-by. Graffiti incised into the central pillar dates back to 1629. Who was the 'TD' who cut his initials? One of the Worth Dollings?

The narrow lancet, in which the writer John Cowper Powys trapped his head, has since been glazed by the stained-glass artist, Alan Younger, who settled nearby. In 1957 a woman's skeleton was found not far from the chapel, beneath a broken Purbeck Marble ledger bearing a cross. Beside her were the foundations of a 2m square building. A solitary anchoress?

The row of cottages, built in 1834, was a barren place of exile for those manning a coastguard station. They moved to Weston in the early 1950s. The Padwicks replaced them, setting up a weaving centre haunted by a St Bernard carrying a donation barrel. When the county planners disapproved his project Mr Padwick painted the row with broad pastille bands, using the ugly result as a sales pitch. During the bitter winter of 1963 he was invalided out by helicopter. The colours faded and the row was sold cheaply to developers. They sold them separately at a huge mark-up. Now all but one are holiday places.

At the end of the Head concrete steps lead to remnants of wartime buildings where low-level radar was developed. I remember passing a rewarding rainy day demolishing the inner walls of one of these, hurling bricks at one side then throwing them all back at the other. Above, a recent bronze sculpture commemorates the men who developed radar here. Another distressing memorial to the Marines, complete with a suburban garden, stands on Emmett Hill. Then there are the stone seats. So many memorials to so many! Isn't the place itself enough?

As boys, we rarely descended the Head by the path followed by the hawser. We preferred Pilot's Path, now thickly, thornily overgrown. Both descend to a long strip of clifftop, bodily slipped, known to Billy Winspit as Ring Bum Gardens. The earliest potatoes in Purbeck grew here and the elder still flowers first. A deep ivy-clad crevasse behind the ledge was home for tawny owls and wood pigeons. It must be the 'Ringbourn' where ten coastguards, greatly outnumbered, killed two smugglers in 1827. Three years later in another confrontation here a smuggler called Bishop was wounded in the neck and not expected to survive. The excisemen lodged him at the pub. Charlie Newman has found several musket balls on the Head.

Pilots Path ran down to Bait-Up, sheltered from southwest winds, where the pilot moored his boat, gazing from the clifftop for likely ships. Descending, he would row out to guide them through the Solent, returning with the next vessel down the Channel. The Solent was a lethal stretch. There, in 1878, my forebear Louis Ferrier was among 300 drowned when the HMS *Eurydice*, almost home from the West Indies, turned turtle. The wife of a Herston quarryman wrote a poem about the wreck and it was one of Winston Churchill's earliest memories. Six months earlier one of Trev's forebears was lost when *The Champion*, carrying 100 tons of stone, went aground in the same area.

For us that route led to the eastern undercliff and from there on along the rocks beneath seabird ledges almost to Crab Hole. At Battery Corner peregrines made an attempt to nest in 1959 before their near-elimination worldwide by dieldrin. We built a hide to watch them: some stones remain. Why Battery Corner? Robinson says of the Head 'near the edge of the cliff were two imitation batteries, one mounting a little iron gun.' Perhaps they were there.

In the 1990s, as they recovered, a pair of peregrines breeding on the west cliffs of the Head repeatedly failed to produce young. Someone had to be taking the eggs or young, valued by Arabs for falconry. A watch was set up. A local Hindu family came at dawn to perform rituals normally requiring the holy Ganges. No one else. Eventually, hatching long overdue, coastguard Jeff Lander volunteered to check the nest. Lowered down, he reported warm eggs in an eyrie full of feathers and racing pigeons' aluminium rings. He brought up the eggs (they were infertile) and a green pigeon ring printed with 'I am lost. Please phone . . .'. Eternally lost.

As kids, we kept a low profile when fishermen such as Sid Lander (Jeff's grandfather) or Bob Harris passed to avoid abuse for taking risks. Once we found a hand grenade washed up under the Head, its pineapple pattern almost worn away! In spring and early summer those eastern cliffs stank of white guano. They were home to shags, herring gulls, guillemots, razorbills and puffins (the last two gone) as well as rock pipits, jackdaws and stock doves. The guillemots no longer 'swarm' as they did when John Bond killed ten in 1822. Lord Eldon would bring 'sportsmen' to shoot them and the fishermen claimed the corpses for bait.

It was enough for us to see them whirring close by, hear their groaning from the cliffs above. The chick leaves in July dusk, its wings too small to fly, with gulls waiting to tear it to pieces. It flutes loudly from above, answering a parent on the sea groaning urgent encouragement. Eventually it flutters down, diving as it hits the water then swimming straight out into the gathering darkness at the tail of its parent. I have hidden beneath the busiest ledge to watch.

The rocks give way to sheer cliff and to go further, to Crab Hole, a nick into the cliff skirted precariously by the footpath, one must swim. It was neither far nor difficult if the tide were slack, dangerous on the ebb. We used to climb up the gap behind a great semi-detached stack we called Bull Rock before learning it was Sutton. It was tricky at the cliff top where the stone was shattered and loose, a relief to clear that rim into the deep grass, cale and sea pinks.

We started swimming off the cliffs at twelve or thirteen, having learned that, given calm weather it was safe close to the rocks between Blackers Hole and Winspit. Once, I pursued a waterlogged young gull off Sutton Rock and was caught in the ebb. I was lucky. In 1935 a youth at Winspit was not. He was never found, but a stone set high on a pile of scars reads: 'He loved birds and green places and the wind on the heath and saw the brightness of the skirt of God'. Some sad soul pushed it over. It stands lower now.

Winspit was being worked in 1719, flourishing in 1756 on Ramsgate work when John Smeaton sought stone for Eddystone Lighthouse. It was the last cliff quarry to function. They say that in the 1930s the man who received the contract to transport stone from Winspit, seeing a good opportunity, invested heavily in a new lorry. Within weeks the company went bust leaving him without work and with big bills. Since it was insured, he pushed the lorry over the cliff and made a claim. The company refused to pay, the policy only covering the truck on the road. Bob Harris revived the quarry during the war and it survived until around 1953. The shells of buildings on the southwest side belong to his time. Without drills, the method of splitting block was a variant of that we used. A row of wedge-shaped 'pits' were punched out along the planned line of fracture and a steel wedge, 'gad', placed in each. They were struck in turn with a 'biddle' until the rock split.

Smeaton says that these quarries were 'to some measure worked underground'. The terrace at Winspit is man-made, comprising the rejected lower, cherty beds. The valuable freestone above was dug out, worked and shipped away leaving a low cliff, which retreated across the terrace. They dug into that face, dragging out block and creating caverns then blasted out the 'legs' supporting the ceiling. This was called a 'founder'. The fallen roof yielded more valuable freestone, the waste was thrown over the cliff

Billy Winspit, William Jeremiah Bower, born here, lived in Winspit cottage all his life, growing vegetables and keeping chickens in his back garden. In front, beside the lawn and fruit trees was his workshop. I remember him showing us his carvings. The dogs and cats were straightforward – a couple of his cats sit by the fireplace at the Square & Compass – but I caused mild offence by mistaking his lizards for crocodiles. He had worked at St Aldhelm's Quarry and Trev used to take him punches and chisels for tempering. In the front room, where we sat whilst Rhoda made tea, was a clock under a glass dome, a stuffed silver pheasant and a browning monochrome print, 'Royal Motherhood', showing the Queen Mother holding baby Elizabeth.

After the First War, when Worth was sold, Billy Winspit was offered his cottage for £250. He replied 'Why should we buy them? Our forefathers built them!' Tenants like him had built on their rented land and held the copyhold for so-many lives. This accounted (in part!) for marriages between ancient men and young girls, since they insured the maximum span of ownership. John Lawrence bought it for him on the understanding that either the debt were repaid or the cottage would pass to him on Billy's death. I forget Rhoda's role in all this, but it seemed a good deal, for they had no children.

When he died in 1966 the weekend fashion was taking off. Houses were no longer homes but commodities. The villages began to die. Winspit cottage was a sign of the times. There was hushed talk in the pub when it sold for a then-incredible £64,000! Local folk can't vie with urban professionals and property speculators. 'Grockles' are something quite different. We are all grockles in one place or another, but it is understandable that weekend cottages burn in Wales. They burned here, too, but differently. A little holiday cottage was set alight in May 1985 as afternoon entertainment for disturbed kids housed near Langton. Trev and I, driving nearby, spotted the pillar of smoke.

Billy never quarried at Winspit. He kept a clinker-built rowing boat down on the shore and did a bit of fishing, hauled a few pots. His family had rights at Seacombe, where he worked until the quarry closed in the 1920s, then again in the '30s when it was briefly active. Mr Davy, manager of the Dorset Quarry Company, first tried to quarry Winspit, investing money and setting up a wooden crane, but he got into a dispute with Col. Strange who had bought the land. Billy suggested he try Seacombe instead, so he towed his crane over there by sea. Mary has photographs showing that same wooden crane being dismantled before the war when her mother bought it from Bob Harris. Its timbers are integrated into the roof of her workshop!

Several times I slept in the last cave along the ledge, disturbed by the regular flash of the lighthouse beam on the ceiling. Puffins nested beneath,

Worbarrow Tout, where Purbeck overlie Portland beds, and Gad Cliff

Ruined Egliston House, once Selina Bond's favourite retreat

Looking from Gad Cliff over Brandy Bay towards St Aldhelm's Head

'Dipper Tom' at the old cliff-side railway at Clavell's Hard; courtesy Dr Phillip Mansel

Chapmans Pool faces a southwest gale

The Golden Bowl - Encombe Valley - towards Fish Wood

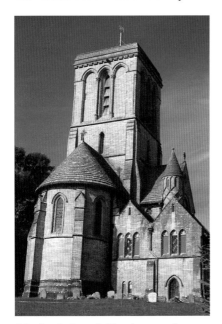

Massive St James' Church, masterly craftsmanship towering over Kingston

Walking up the scarp to new St James's Church; courtesy Dr Philip Mansel

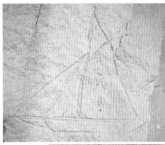

Celtic fields;
Pier Bottom

A 19th century
sailing vessel cut
into the cliff

Crane at St Aldhelm's Quarry

Low spring tide and a heavy shower from
Rope Lake to St Aldhelm's Head

The Seacombe cliff-fall of 1992 threatens to
engulf Watch Rock

View from Worth with lynchets on the flank of West Man

St Nicholas of Myra, Worth Matravers

Mirror recovered from the Halsewell wreck in 1786

A lancet below two carved corbels

Purbeck puffin

Guillemots perch on a rock, once our cliff-top view-point; Durlston

Juvenile razorbill off the cliffs

Young Puffin; photo Richard Verge

Watch Rock and the inlet where boats came for stone from the quarry above

Southeasterly gale hits the coast near Cunner Cove

Swanage Bay today

The paddlesteamer Waverley *pulls out of Swanage pier*

Swanage Bay in 1941, anti-invasion 'dragon's teeth' and scaffolding; photo James Jeffries

St George's First School maypole dancing at Langton Fete at Durnford

St George's Church with Mary Spencer Watson's millennium figure, Purbeck Quarryman

Headstones in Langton's old cemetery

gathering in a little knot offshore on June evenings. Beyond my cave the cliff is briefly sheer before another narrow quarried ledge. That has been called Halsewell since 1786. On fine summer days a boat or two of divers is usually moored off it.

The *Halsewell*, an East Indiaman of 758 tons, set sail for Calcutta on 1st January 1786. She ran into a gale bearing snow, and soon sprung a leak. The Captain, Richard Pierce, making his last trip, was taking two daughters with him. Perhaps he hoped to marry them favourably in the booming capital of British India. They sighted Berry Head but were forced back up the Channel. Pierce hoped to make Portsmouth for repairs but in the first hours of 6th January the *Halsewell* was driven straight towards that cliff, hit the rocks and fell on her side. According to tradition the survivors climbed, or hid behind, the huge leaning rock that remains in the undercliff. Some reached the clifftop. Black Man's Stile marks the spot where a 'black man' - perhaps he was Indian - collapsed and died after escaping the wreck.

Dramatic prints portray the captain in the roundhouse, his arms about his daughters. Three black women and two soldiers wives joined them, but it did them little good. The ship broke up rapidly. At daybreak people from Worth, summoned by survivors came with ropes. 82 men survived. Of the 168 who died, those washed up lie buried in Seacombe Bottom. By the time the vicar rode out to inspect the scene, fragments of the ship littered the sea, interspersed with chairs, tables and casks. Inside Worth church, above the door is a small wood-framed mirror saved from the wreck.

The East India Company sent 100 guineas reward to be distributed to the people of Worth. The Square and Compass museum has one silver shilling from that bounty along with other objects recovered by divers. Trev has a flintlock from the wreck. The tragedy was sufficiently notorious to cause George III to visit the site. Incised in the quarry face are several outlines of ships, one claimed to represent the *Halsewell*. That story is recent and drawings of passing vessels or the craft that carried the stone, are quite common. Five years ago, in Calcutta's Park Street Cemetery I came upon the headstone of Mr Pierce, 'son of the master of the *Halsewell*', and immediately that stretch of cliff, the sea at its fiercest, sprung to mind.

In 1982 a gentler disaster took place nearby. David Strange, working the field above, joined the other men for tea. Later, one of the men asked 'Where is the tractor?'. Quietly and unnoticed it had glided 100 metres through the fence to shatter on the rocks below. Its rusting ruins lay amongst them for several years afterwards.

Seacombe stands where the coastline turns to run eastwards. Celia Fiennes: 'At a place 4 miles off (from Quarr Farm) called Sea Cume the rockes are so craggy and creekes of land so many that the sea is very turbulent, there I picked shells and it being a spring tide I saw the sea beat upon the rockes at least 20 yards with such a foam or froth, and at another place the rockes had so large a cavity and hollow that when the sea flowed in it runne almost around, and sounded like some hall or high arch." But it was a very different Seacombe she saw, the narrow valley as yet unquarried , the western hillside running uninterrupted to the sea.

A 1772 map of Worth differentiates between Purbeck stone 'Paviour Quarries' and Portland stone 'Freestone Quarries'. Seacombe, dug as at Winspit, became one of the largest of the latter. Cliffstone became fashionable in the 18th century, used in Wareham Manor House (1712) and the rebuilding of Encombe House (1736). Apart from contributing to Ramsgate harbour, Seacombe stone built the Encombe obelisk, the clock house of Dover Pier, Winchester Prison, West India Docks, lighthouses at Margate and the Isle of Wight and many Dorset churches and bridges.

Beneath the quarry, difficult to reach except at extreme low tide, the west end of the sea-level terrace was a 'dock' where stone boats came alongside to load. Sockets cut into the living rock show where lifting gear stood. One block, known as Loading Rock, was washed over into the sea in 1978. Another, Watch Rock, isolated on a sea ledge and featured in old sketches of the place, owes its name to the fact that the height of the water on it indicated whether a boat could dock. At the quarry's last stage, stone left Seacombe by lorry. On the grassy terrace concrete foundations of saws remain and the soil is impregnated with cinders from the steam engines that powered them. Pieces of heavy machinery still rust amongst the rocks below.

The underground workings survive, the older ones onto the side of the valley hidden behind banks of waste. Fenced off when the National Trust took over, there was even talk of foundering them. It was all open for us boys, cattle sheltering there leaving the floor rich in dung. Usually a Little Owl sat in a crack above a loose block about to fall: the block still waits but the owl has gone.

The largest rock fall in my memory, in 1992, blocked off one of the two sea caves, Michael's and William's (I am never sure which is which), after a National Trust employee was using a pile driver to knock in fence posts. At first the fan of rubble reached Watch Rock but it has broken up to form a new pebble beach.

Overlooking the mouth of Seacombe valley from the east is a large dome of rusty steel, an Allen Williams Steel Turret, this could rotate. It was designed to house several different gun types ready to great the invaders that never came. A footpath running up the western valley and over the ridge leads to Worth Matravers.

WORTH MATRAVERS

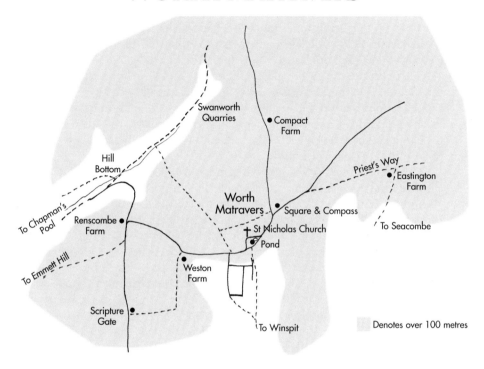

The once-flourishing village of Worth Matravers gazes down a lynchet-terraced valley towards the sea. Worth is said to mean both 'dwelling' and 'shore' but it features as 'Orde' in Domesday. Elsewhere that signifies 'point' or 'headland'. Brief late 14th century ownership of the manor by the Maltravers of Lychett supplied the suffix. In ecclesiastical terms it was more important than Swanage, its church serving a chapel there until 1506. The priest commuted along 'Priest's Way'.

The parish runs as a narrow strip from the sea down into the valley to embrace Dunshay, the manor house for the village. Dunshay's famous son, Benjamin Jesty, though native of Yetminster was buried in Worth churchyard in 1816. He regularised the art of vaccination, inoculating his wife and children with fluid drawn from the pustules of a cow-pox infected cow. The significance was soon apparent. A memorial on the north wall of the church states that the deceased's mother 'was personally inoculated for cow pox by

Benjamin Jesty'. His contemporary, Jenner, a better self-publicist, took most of the credit for vaccination. Soon it was common practice but total eradication took many years. When I started travelling in Asia in the mid-sixties kids and adults blinded, white-eyed and horribly scarred by the disease were commonplace.

The Dolling family held Worth into the late eighteenth century. In 1793 the Calcrafts of Rempstone bought it. The village received a certain independence in 1919 when Captain Marston inherited the estate from Mrs Calcraft then sold off Worth. Col. John Strange acquired the farmland. Tenants with the means bought their cottages and Worth lost the patronage of a squire. But there was a negative effect. Generally the large estates are keener to rent than to sell and post-feudal policy is often sympathetic to the local community. That Worth became a weekend village, thus died, was due to that great sale. Margaret Thatcher added to the crisis by selling off council houses.

The village might have survived if planners had put people above prettiness, allowing and regulating more affordable building. Worth had a history of 'temporary homes'. In 1920 Great Western Railway sold off a dozen railway carriages at £25 a piece. Dragged by horses up Kingston Hill, they became a feature of the village. Sid Lander's, below the village, was said to be 1st class. Most have gone now, but Charlie Newman cherishes one. Prefabricated temporary military quarters at Weston, unaltered, provided homes long after peace came. Joan Begbie did her bit to temper the clearances. Long settled in Worth, she became a familiar, popular figure, her herd of Jack Russells constantly losing themselves down badgers' setts. She wrote several books on the countryside and, sensitive to the dilemma, left land specifically for affordable housing, thus Begbie Cottages.

Historically, Worth thrived on three main occupations: agriculture, the extraction and working of stone and fishing. The early 19th century battle against smugglers brought a large coastguard staff into the parish. Censuses mark its decline as smuggling decreased. In 1841 there were 14 coastguards as against 20 masons/quarrymen but by 1871 only 8 coastguards to 21 stoneworkers.

Today, only the Square and Compass, situated to hold its head high over its neighbours makes Worth more than another pretty, manicured holiday village. Originally two cottages, it became one, the central porch fashioned of stone slabs said to come from East Man. It may have opened as a pub in the early 1700s under the name of The Two Hammers. Referred to as The Sloop in a sale document of April 1833 it acquired the present name during that changeover, reflecting the new manager's trade. Charles Bower appears in censuses as both publican and stone-cutter. A broken stone found at the pub also names him as 'Licensed to sell Tea, Tobacco and Snuff'.

Worth reached its zenith in the 1920s and '30s. Then, still a lively agricultural and quarrying village, it became fashionable amongst a set of creative folk. Artists and writers frequented the pub, run by another Charlie Newman, the present landlord's great grandfather. Augustus John, living in Poole, was a regular. Leslie Banks and Gwen Ffranccon Davies were amongst the actors who dropped in. Both used to take Lobster Cottage, beside the church. No doubt the painter Frances Hodgkins, living in Worth before she moved to Corfe, visited the Square. Some of that inter-war clientele left their work behind. There is a large Leon Heron cartoon of closing time, an Augustus John pencil sketch of the prewar Charlie Newman and a cartoon of Augustus John by David Low. Basil Stump's portrait of Billy Winspit appeared on the wall after his death in 1966 and we bemoaned its glaring colours. Decades passing, so much tobacco has produced a yellow patina, softening it into an Old Master.

During the war a new, no less lively clientele came from the RAF camp. Some of the tables still bear graffiti, including someone's 'VE Day 1945'. With peace, a few of the art circle drifted back half-heartedly and briefly The writer, Laurie Lee, took up residence for a few months.

By the early sixties, when I started to drink there 'The Square' was very much a village local. Eileen Newman had taken over when her father died in 1953, five years after her brother drowned. She served a pint of rough cider at 10d (not much over 4p), cheap even then. Famous faces still appeared. Free of any security, Michael Stewart, Labour Foreign Secretary, would come with his wife for a quiet drink, running the gauntlet of the staunchly-Tory regulars in the entrance corridor. They made *sotto voce* remarks as he passed.

Raymond and Stella Newman took over from Eileen in 1973, moving up to Worth from The King's Arms in Langton. I knew both well. As a child, my mother once sat me on the counter at a grocer's shop in Swanage next to a stacked triangle of tins. I removed the bottom one, just to see... The resultant shock stays with me. Stella, new on the staff, was sweet about it and I remembered her with affection ever after. Sadly, she died in 1976.

Relations with Raymond as publican were more awkward. His long-respectable hobby, egg-collecting, was to be outlawed by the Bird Protection Act, and I belonged to a small gang of boys who, having tasted bird-nesting turned to conservation. Far more of our generation were egg-collectors. During the spring, whilst they patrolled the cliffs carrying ropes, we carried binoculars. Raymond seemed the greatest threat. An excellent climber, he was rarely defeated by a cliff or a tree. Every year he would get the peregrine and raven eggs, as well as those of sea birds and other rarities. By the time he took over the pub he had retired from climbing but it was a couple of years before we talked about his eggs. Then one evening he told little Charlie (always clad in blue dungarees in those days) to take me upstairs and show off his collection, built up in the early fifties and stored in drawers divided by wooden partitions, a little cotton-wool nest for each clutch of eggs. Beautiful, dead things, most represented an adventure, hours of watching until the bird betrayed its nest, risky climbs.

He spoke of some of those climbs. We had seen him at others. He usually managed to take the Purbeck peregrines' eggs although they sometimes succeeded at Anvil Point. Had he never been scared? Then he talked of an eyrie at Swyre Head - the one beyond Durdle Door. Alone, tying a rope to a strong fence-post he had gone over the high chalk cliff. The eyrie was over halfway down in a slight overhang but by swinging in he had reached it and taken the clutch. A tiring business, he now faced a dilemma. The rope was much too short to descend to the shingle beach below, the jump from its end far to risky. His only option was to climb straight up. Hanging free, at first there was no support to grip onto and rest. It was his worst struggle, getting back up. He thought he would never make it. Later, I gave him a photograph taken as he climbed to a sparrowhawks' nest in Little Linnings Wood. We were hidden in bushes beneath, watching.

Raymond had other interests, collecting fossils and archaeological objects as well as eggs. Apart from the eggs, Charlie also took to collecting, encouraged in the fossils by David Sole who himself developed it into a fine art. His museum at the end of the pub, based on his father's collection, is remarkable. When he and Sarah Loudoun took over running the Square on his father's death in 1993 they were tenant landlords as his great-grandfather had been in 1907. Charlie bought the freehold the following year and revitalised the pub, making music an important feature. He launched an autumn Pumpkin Festival, when all manner of pumpkins are displayed. It is competitive; the largest winning its grower a prize. He also took over the stone carving fortnight, originally a neglected part of Swanage Carnival, and launched an annual Square Fair to coincide.

The view from the Square is remarkable. On very clear nights like that of the Square Fair in August 2004 it is possible to see the lights of Cherbourg. There is always lively debate whether these are real or some optical trick of refraction. Having originally favoured the former, Pete convinced me it was the latter. No one disagrees that the source is France.

Once the church was the village hub. Now, a single rector in Langton serves Worth and Kingston, also taking the occasional service, the marriages, at St Aldhelm's Head. It remains the most prominent feature but the world has changed with material wealth and comfort. The sacred site is much older than the present building. Burials from the first Christian centuries have been discovered in the churchyard. Nevertheless, St Nicholas of Myra (Father Christmas, from Myra, off the Turkish coast - a popular dedicatee in

The Square and Compass emblem; a pumpkin

the 11th century) is one of the oldest churches in Dorset, handsome in its dog-tooth Norman chancel arch never intended for the building. It doesn't fit the surrounding fabric, being designed for a larger church. Worn corbels on the north and south walls depict human and animal heads, a pair of hares beside a cat. The battered tympanum above the door bears a relief of the coronation of the virgin and on its back, within the church, is that decorated mirror from the *Halsewell*.

The pyramidal tower roof, so much part of the silhouette, was only added in 1869.

The rectory with its high wall, built for priests who were not as common folk, was sold to become a private house after the war. The tenants' children were at the grammar school with me and as a boy I shot a rook from the conical-roofed gazebo in its wall. The wounded bird flew on to fall dead amongst the vegetables in the allotments. The turret remains, its windows taken from some mediaeval building, but where are the allotments, the folk that worked them?

Worth village lived into our times. There were two shops. In 1913 the Pushmans took over the one opposite the pond, holding the post office. John Pushman, always in spotted bow tie, presided there, aided by Ron Samways. Now it is under threat. The other was in Calico Cottage. It stands below the school, closed in 1921, which is now the village hall. Village kids moved to St George's School. A number of the cottages were still held by folk who worked the land, quarried or fished or had retired from such work. Old working men in caps and waistcoats sat out in the sun. We could refill our water bottles at the village pump, the main source of water until the mains supply arrived in 1965. It was later sealed, retained as 'heritage' then stolen as antique. Near it, fed by the same spring as the pond, is the withy bed, gazed upon by Mike Bizley's gatepost owls. The willows, grown huge, no longer provide the wands for weaving lobster and prawn pots.

I lived in Worth briefly in the early seventies, taking tiny Blue Skies, later demolished and rebuilt less tiny. While out at work I rarely locked it, often coming home to find some friend already having tea. It had neither running water nor sewage connection. A lorry came round to empty our 'elsans' and I drew water from a covered spring just up the track. Miss Bacon, known as the Lady Gardener, had lived there. Some mornings, on our way to work, we passed her towing the tools of her trade in one of those little shopping baskets on wheels. A friendly, gentle character, a returned Anglo-Argentine, she shifted to Acton where she died surrounded by cats.

Harry Samways, Ron's brother, lived in the cottage on the double bend at Weston, now called Old Harry after him. Sometimes, in his old mac, trousers tucked into wellington boots, he would recline on the Green in the sunshine, his legs half across the road. One day, he lost the door key, so he came and went through a window. Weeks later, when an injury to his foot gave trouble a nurse at the hospital took off his boots and found the key lodged undisturbed in one of them.

A Worth hobby was voyeurism, using binoculars to follow couples from some clifftop vantage point. Invariably they provided entertainment. At first, I mistook this for an enthusiasm for ornithology: we view the world through a narrow perspective. I was soon disabused. Tony Viney, writing the obituary of one familiar voyeur put it something like this: 'we can think of him now, looking down on us from above.'

If the shop threatens to close, the café thrives on a burgeoning tourist trade. Passing it after work at the quarry we joked at the expense of the movable sign outside. What would be 'today's special'? On it, white on black and unchanged for years, was written 'Today's Special – Crab'. The menu has branched out now, drawing more punters into the pretty garden. Next to it, Val Quinn's figures of St Nicholas look down from the gateposts. The pond nearby, fed by the spring, supplied beasts with drinking water in the days of horse transport and freely-moving cattle. Ducks have upended there for years, briefly absent in 1989 when someone complained of them as a road hazard and the owner slew the lot in protest. The complaint was negative: at their own risk, they earn praise as traffic calmers.

As long as the RAF camp operated Worth was lively. The body of the camp was south of the road to Renscombe Farm, where the modern tied cottages stand. It comprised asbestos-sheet huts and tall timber pylons surrounded by a high black-painted metal fence. It was abandoned, the timber pylons dismantled, in 1960. Exploring the empty huts, we came upon murals - views of Corfe, Swanage, of the farm opposite - with which the bored inhabitants had decorated their walls. The tallest pylon, made of steel, rose above the present Adventure Centre (housed in the original huts). That survived much longer. On 23rd August 1975, hearing that it was to come down, Trev and I climbed to the top, looking out over 'A fantastic view of Purbeck and beyond - to the west sunbeams broke through the clouds and struck the sea and coast around Durdle Door.' Next day I returned with a camera. When halfway up, Pete Cuffe, one of the farm-workers from the tied cottages, shouted. Instead of doing the wise thing - continuing up and facing the music afterwards - I descended. The pylon was felled soon afterwards, so I never got those views.

Since 1919 the principal farmers have been the Stranges, but they earned other fame. Between the wars, Col Louis Strange, an ex-air ace, founded the Purbeck Light Aeroplane Club. He took off from the village and a field behind the pub is still known as 'Aerodrome'. Hettie, now Dr Heather Elgood, is an expert of South Asian painting. We meet at Indian events in London. Her brother, David, couples farming with astronomy, being generous with the large telescope he has set up.

The James family farmed Renscombe under Encombe Estate from 1926 to 1995. In the 1960s Mrs James served the best cream teas. The farm house and its barns may be old, but the settlement, once under the Abbey of Cerne, is far older. There is a 19th century story that while replacing a staircase in the south side of the farmhouse a tiny cell was revealed containing the skeleton of a woman. There is mention of shreds of cassock, a crucifix. When Renscombe sold in the 1990s its fate was certain: holiday accommodation under one guise or another. It has been smartened up and laid to rest. Beyond it the road runs down to Hill Bottom, once a hamlet of fishing and farming people. Near there, beneath the rookery, I saw my only wind-blown milkweed butterfly, the American monarch.

The most important quarry in Worth is Swanworth, formerly Sheepslights. Some say the old name derived from Ships' Lights, talking of a romantic glimpse down the valley towards lights at sea. It is more prosaic but more likely that it was either a 'plot for grazing sheep' or the dumping place for dead livestock and their parts. David Pushman, whose father, Jack (brother of John at the shop) worked there for 55 years, has written a booklet on the quarry's history. It began in the 1900s as a small quarry worked by two men but Worth Quarries Ltd took it over in 1923. Specialising in crushed stone for hardcore, it rose quickly to employ 50 men. Swanworth Quarries Ltd took over in the early 1930s, then Tarmac in 1980 but the hardcore continued to flow, metalling roads and reclaiming land near Poole Quay. Planning laws dictate that the great pit it created will never enrich the landscape. It must be manicured back into safe suburban tidiness.

Eastington Farm, just off Priest's Way, was run as rough pasture by the Curtis family. There were two brothers and a sister, all unmarried, which never seems so strange amongst farming folk. Their work, giving little leisure, tends to isolate them from the community. There are tales of their milk cheques piling up, uncashed on the mantelpiece, of a large bagful of bank notes falling off the trailer when they finally moved out of the farm. That was after Ralph Bankes died in 1981 and the estate passed to The National Trust. As tenants, the Curtises had let the 17th century farmhouse and outbuildings fall into decline. Eastington's fate was sealed: urban wealth was the easy way to restore it so it became another holiday place. As it was being done-up in one room a patch of contemporary wall painting was discovered under layers of plaster.

From Eastington a broad track, now a footpath, winds down into the east fork of the Seacombe valley, passing a spring where sheep were once dipped. The remnants of an enclosure is lost in brambles. Above the spring are three elongated pillow mounds, structures which puzzle archaeologists. Probably mediaeval, both Purbeck sets (the other being above Church Knowle) are similarly placed just above the spring-line. This was the road that served Seacombe Quarry and it runs down to cross the clifftop path to Swanage.

SEACOMBE TO PEVERIL POINT

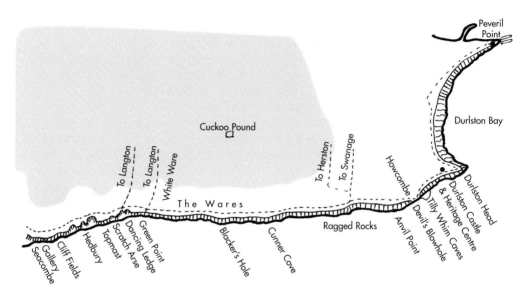

Denotes over 100 metres

Two forks of Seacombe valley, from Eastington and from Abbascombe meet to run as one to the sea, crossing the cliff path, narrow and lightly worn in the fifties. Even of a summer weekend it was unusual to see an unfamiliar face. Another Ice Age-formed valley, Seacombe leads onto a sea-level platform that has become a popular swimming place in summer. Twenty years ago ageing Vic Bower of Worth told me how he had tried swimming there as a boy. The cold water constricting his chest put him off. He never went in again. He was to die with his face in primroses. There are worse ways. On the east a cave of deep water prevents access to the continuing ledge below Gallery quarry. A precarious path leads from the top of the cliff down to Gallery from which, until a cliff fall, it was easy to climb down to sea level. The low cliffs beyond are known as Cliff Fields.

A horizontal bed, eroded out as a prominent feature along most of the cliff between St Aldhelm's Head and Durlston forms the nesting ledge for many of Purbeck's sea-birds. At Cliff Fields, that ledge is low. There were several puffin sites here where, by gripping the ledge and doing a pull-up, we boys could look in at a sitting puffin or, later, a fluffy puffling. The story of Dorset puffins has been one of permanent decline. In our lifetime, save for a handful in Portland (a single pair now, I am told) the only Dorset puffins were in Purbeck. In 1818 John Bond of Creech pointed out that they '...build more to the West about Lulworth' so he went there to shoot them. They seem to have gone from there well before the end of that century. Shooting sea-birds was popular and you could hire a boat for the pleasure. It was not always a one way game. In 1834 the curate of Langton, living with his father in Magnolia House in Swanage High Street, set off with his brother to sail to Dancing Ledge, intending to shoot 'sea-gulls'. By accident he shot himself in the arm and died a few weeks later.

Such 'sportsmen' and the collection of eggs for food helped the puffin's decline but more important are diminishing food supplies and climate change. They seem certain to vanish before long. In the late 1950s of a late June evening we might see between 50 and 60 just west of Dancing Ledge and they were thinly distributed from Battery Corner to Durlston, with a gap along Ragged Rocks. By 1963 they had disappeared from Cliff Fields and Durlston. Now a few hold on at one site. But there is profit against the loss. More birds have colonised Purbeck in my lifetime than have left it, amongst them egrets, collared doves and Cetti's warblers.

At the eastern end of Cliff Fields, accessible only from the sea, is Pig'n'Whistle, so named because a little blowhole hisses out a spray of water with every wave. Beyond it a stream flows over a short, sheer stretch of cliff before West Hedbury.

Hedbury, amongst the largest cliffstone quarries, was still active at the end of the 19th century. Divided into West and East, the name derived from the Eidbury family who opened the quarry in the mid 18th century. The path down to the smaller, western part still passes over a stone sunk in the ground holding the socket for a pulley wheel. From West Hedbury the quarried terrace narrows as a little shelf to stop abruptly at a pile of rubble just short of East Hedbury. Over this remnant of a fallen ceiling is a large, dark cave, its ceiling precarious in parts, formed by quarrying. This leads to East Hedbury.

People refer to East Hedbury as 'Cannon Cove' for the rusty gun that lies here, more defence against Napoleon. For most of its life it rested half-sunken on a pile of scars, sometimes buried from sight. Then in the mid 1970s the Langton Preservation Society raised it on a plinth. They say it was primed to fire a crow-bar at a French privateer. History doesn't record with what success.

Beneath the quarry a deep sea cave runs into the cliff. This was a good place to bring stone boats alongside for loading and above it are traces of the crane that lowered stone to be stacked on a ledge ready for fine weather and the next boat. Philip Brannon, author of several 1850s guidebooks, refers to a natural cavern hereabouts as Connaught's Hole. Many of the recorded cliff names were extracted from Billy Winspit over a bottle of whisky. Did Brannon mean this or another further east, which Billy called Cunner Cove? The Hedbury cave was the more important, if less visible feature.

High to the east of Hedbury is a small precarious quarry which Billy Winspit called Topmast, saying that a ship had hit the cliff here with such force that its topmast broke off and landed on the ledge. Looking at the place, that is impossible. There is a similar, authentic tale of the *Alexandrovna* wreck of 1882 where a topmast landed more feasibly on the clifftop near the Measured Mile markers. Perhaps the name, as good as any, reflects its high position on the cliff; perhaps it reflects that whisky.

The next quarry of any size, Scratch Arse, lies halfway between Hedbury and Dancing Ledge. The origin of the name is uncertain and every suggestion seems improbable. Guillemots and Puffins used to breed on the ledge opposite. Once, late in the season, we climbed up there from a boat to look at the well-fledged puffin. Richard aimed his camera into the darkness and was lucky. That may be the only photograph of a Purbeck puffin chick.

There is another tiny precarious quarry called Platter before Dancing Ledge. From there we could climb down and get a good view of the auks breeding in Bird Cove, a shallow cave nearby. No one need make that effort now. Beside the path is an ugly metal cupboard-like object connected to a video camera focussed all summer on the ledge. Presumably one can sit, warm and comfy in the building at Durlston and watch that same ledge. Thank god I was born too early!

But I have another reason to remember Platter. As a fourteen-year-old looking for my friends, I climbed down there to find a young couple stark naked and hard at work. Never having seen anything of that sort before, I retreated unnoticed and, standing on the top of the cliff, craned over to watch. I learned a lot. The following Sunday at tea at Ulwell Farm Mrs Verge said, 'We went up to Dancing Ledge last weekend and saw you looking over the clifftop. There must have been some interesting bird there. What was it?' Turning scarlet, I talked of puffins. It seemed little more than the truth.

In early July 1957 a sailing boat, the *Arctic Dawn* sprang a serious leak and went down in fine weather off the coast near Dancing Ledge. The two men who rowed ashore talked of their treasures left on board. We mourned their good binoculars (we then shared a battered pair of my father's) but there was no way of retrieving them. The top of the mast remained for some time tantalisingly visible at low tide. That summer was a spectacular one for mackerel, the sea at Dancing Ledge hissing as the sand eels they pursued desperately broke water. Some boys caught them with nothing more than a bit of silver paper on a hook. The eels, driven by panic, glistened and died on the rocks.

Dancing Ledge closed as a quarry before WWI. A double track punched out for, then worn smooth by the wheels of laden stone carts still runs from the top of the ledge to the deep water at its edge. There a crane stood to load worked stone onto boats. A few Langton folk swam here. The bravest youths jumped, even dived, from the quarry level into the deep water west of the Ledge. In 1893 Thomas Pellatt, headmaster of Langton's Durnford school commissioned the cutting of a swimming pool for his pupils. A couple of iron pegs were embedded in the rock to hold a metal grating, locked against the *hoipoloi*. Admiral Tovey, a Durnford pupil, during his Langton old age commented that he had been scarred for life when washed against that grating. The sea made short shrift of it. Those boys were not mollycoddled. James Pembroke remembers that even in the mid seventies he was left to fend for himself in the sea beyond the ledge.

By our time the pool was open to all. Kids stuck to it but we older boys only used it in rough weather when big waves rush up to boil into the pool. Gripping an iron peg on the seaward side we would face them. Let go and you twirled around a couple of times in the white water, washing-machine like, before snatching a breath.

Spyway School adopted the pool when Durnford closed. Each winter the sea sweeps rubble into it and, rarely, it was pumped dry as the spring tide receded. We helped clear it under Spyway in May 1964, then under The Old Malthouse in June 1995. It is always an event. Each time something interesting turns up, a conger eel amongst the fish, a small lobster, a crab or two.

In the fifties boys with ropes appeared in springtime. They were the opposing team, boys of our generation who collected eggs. We had that adventurous country life in common and I am now on good terms with several of them. I had collected too, but by then only took herring gulls' and rooks' eggs - one from each contrasting clutch. Nests were a challenge and eggs such beautiful things. The large guillemot's egg is particularly striking, long and pointed so that it rolls in a circle, not over the cliff. Although usually dark-blotched on a bright turquoise ground they vary considerably. One, confiscated, stood on the windowsill in the headmaster's study, sole consolation for a summons there.

Climbing for its own sake didn't start until the late 1960s. Climbers, outsiders with bright ropes and clinking equipment, soon became a feature of the cliffs. We took them as intruders, interfering as they did with nesting birds, sticking metal pegs into the grassy clifftop, trespassing on our world. There weren't many at first and Richard Crewe, author of the first book on Purbeck climbs, was their doyen. Attending their good parties rather compromised me. It was like racism, only sustainable in ignorance and most

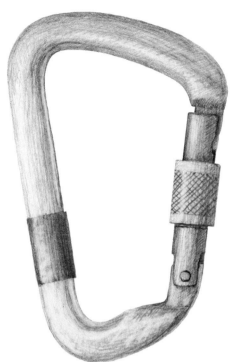

A guillemot's egg; a climber's caribina

of the climbers were pleasant and reasonable. They leave sad traces, however, bright little loops that mark out routes or trophies to celebrate another climb conquered. Godless, I understand the concept of desecration. By 1975 an agreement defined areas to be closed for climbing during the breeding season. Most climbers respect them.

East of Dancing Ledge, Green Point is made so by a streamlet, which waters green algae over an ever-extending deposit of lime tufa. Beyond it an abrupt dry valley, Whiteware, ends in midair. The Wares is the sloping grassland and scrub from ridge to clifftop, much of it uneven from quarrying. The poor alkaline soil supports a rich limestone flora, spectacular are spider orchids in April and sparser bee orchids in June.

Rocks form an undercliff from Green Point almost as far as Blackers Hole. One almost ten metres long, a great table-like platform, half-submerged, fell not thirty years back. There are several small quarried ledges along this stretch. Of a pair one above the other east of Whiteware each exploits a valuable freestone bed. The footpath used to continue directly eastwards, curving into a steep scoop into the slope. Heavy rains in the autumn of 1960 set the topsoil moving above this scoop. The whole surface slipped, sending earth and vegetation over the cliff, discolouring the sea with a tail of sediment. Ever since the path has diverted around the place, returning to the clifftop above Blackers Hole, a high cavern showing darkly from many points west along the coast. It is the only place in Purbeck where Kittiwakes still nest. Was there a Blacker? I know nothing of him. Some say it was Black Arse Hole. A Victorian writer primly suggests Blackguard's Hole. Recent rockfalls make the descent dangerous. Herring gulls nest there, laying their first eggs as do guillemots around St George's Day. I used to swim into the cave early in the laying season, the eggs fresh and the sea cold, to bring eggs out in the knotted sleeves of my shirt.

Two tall pylons above the cliff, placed exactly a nautical mile from another pair at Durlston are used for speed trials, naval ships measuring their time between pairs. Below, the ground slopes to a low cliff of solid rock falling sheer into deep water, only broken by a cave at its eastern end. That is Cunner Cove. An odd formation gives the effect of stage-curtains looped up at its entrance. The climbers call it 'Deep Water Solo' and attempt to climb over it without ropes, relying on the deep water to break their fall.

That sheer face smashes breakers in a southeasterly, sending a burst of spray high up into the air. It is my favorite place on a rough day. Recently, Pete and I walked there in an amazing downpour carried on a furious gale to watch the waves. We called this stretch *Alexandrovna* after a 1250 ton sailing ship that struck further east in April 1882. She was spotted, sails shredded, running with a gale straight for the cliff. By the time help arrived there was only smashed wreckage drifting on the tide towards Swanage. It was here that the top few feet of one of the masts was found in the grass. All twenty of the crew drowned. Some are buried in Swanage churchyard. Five days later, the sea calm, a steamer brought sightseers to view the wreckage.

In our time only one timber, a stubby upright near Cunner Cove, remained of the cranes used for lowering stone. It disappeared in the early 1960s. From there to Anvil Point stretches Ragged Rocks, boulders lining the foot of, for us, an unproductive stretch of cliff, passed to get elsewhere. Anvil Point and Durlston stand in contrast. Hillcrest, my prep school, was not far away so it was on school walks here that I first saw guillemots and puffins. We were taken inside the lighthouse to watch as a warning charge (long ago replaced by the wailing siren) was fired. We came here, too, as a crocodile of blue-blazered brats to watch another solar eclipse through black negatives. We sat on the hillside to glimpse, so faintly through haze *Britannia* bearing the new Queen back from her royal tour met by her last battleship, HMS *Vanguard*. They took us to Howcombe Cove beside Tilly Whim, with its Devil's Blowhole where a blast of air roars up with each big wave. Given the right conditions it performs spectacularly, as on the stormy 16th January 1974: 'At Tilly Whim the sea was breaking up over the ledge and...the blowhole was functioning, driving a column of spray into the air.' In calmer weather we caught 'bunners' in the rock pools there whilst guillemots circled off Anvil Point, named for an anvil-shaped block beneath it.

The seabird colonies at Durlston were the most accessible for us Swanage boys. In Spring we often cycled up after school. From a projecting point of rock halfway between Tilly Whim Caves and the high-walled lookout point we could count the birds on the main Guillemot ledge and watch their progress. Razorbills bred on the side of that point and fulmars hovered close by to examine us. Passing walkers commented on the insecurity of our perch in the timid way of adulthood. It was solid enough, even if the crack between it and the main clifftop discernibly widened. Then one day in the mid 1960s it was gone, a jumble of rocks in the sea below.

In the sixties and seventies Dave Sales, descended from the Gibbons, one of two fishing families in Studland, keen on birds, used to take us along the cliff in an annual seabird count. He also kept us up to date with interesting birds he spotted out at sea when hauling his pots. Later that coastal trip became a commercial venture.

In 1973 Dorset County Council bought the area and it became Durlston Country Park. Tilly Whim Caves were left open for several years until after a rock-fall they were closed for fear of litigation. With the death of God, man's fate is measured in common currency and there is usually someone to sue. Tilly Whim is derived from a Mr Tilly who set up a 'whim', a local lifting device. 'Whim' is archaic now. On the map in Mary's copy of Hutchins' *History of Dorset* someone has inked in his tacking track from Weymouth to Lulworth in 1802. The vessel was *The Whim*, but there are whims and whims. There was a small charge to descend into the caves. The gate was closed by evening so we climbed over the wall.

There is a reference to Tilly Whim in 1703. The quarry flourished during the 18th century boom and stone for Portsmouth's fortifications probably came from here. A list of Tilly Whim's output from 1805-10 includes numbers of pairs of staddle stones, half-peck sinks and troughs, the feet of rollers, tons of pitchers and block. Two years later its output was much reduced and it succumbed to lack of demand in 1820. Blocks from the ceiling standing in the quarry are unusual in being a mass of oyster shells.

We would climb down to sea level, scramble along the rocks underneath the grassy slope where puffins bred and swim beneath the guillemot colonies. Without disturbing the birds, we could also climb up onto the main guillemot ledge, emerging behind a rock.

Kittiwakes began nesting at Durlston in the 1950s, raising young in 1956. Increasing each year, they established secondary colonies east of St Aldhelm's

Head and at Blackers Hole. They quit Durlston in 1994, affected by the reappearance of peregrines. I have seen a young peregrine slaughter and eat a young kittiwake at its nest whilst its sibling stood curiously by. Durlston is the nucleus of local fulmars, too, where we first saw eggs and young. At the extreme edge of their range, they come, flirt but few breed. Dolphins (as 'porpoises') feature in my diary entries for Durlston, sometimes, even allowing for exaggeration, in large numbers. 29th March 1956: 'We saw a huge school of porpoises a few miles long.'

East of the guillemot ledge herring gulls nest on our 'Easy Ledge', simple to raid. Across a shallow cave is another, bigger, 'Hard Ledge' which I first reached in May 1957. We never used ropes. The trick for the first, overhanging part of the descent to the Hard Ledge was to slide down a rusty pipe projecting from concrete at the clifftop. Returning, you leaned back against it. That pipe remains but, rusted through, it has fallen sideways. Off to one side of the climb was a little chamber in the cliff, slightly walled. Trev's father said a man lived somewhere here between the wars, raiding nearby gardens for vegetables and chickens. Surely too small and rough-floored for that, it is better to think of a few kegs stored there when smuggling liquor was a major industry.

George Burt's name looms large over Durlston. He launched the first country park, moulding the landscape to suit his fancy. Tilly Whim as a romantic smuggling site, the clifftop walk above Durlston Bay, the Zigzag path down to it, the Great Globe and the gothick castle were his creation. So were the inscribed quotes, the improving statistics he scattered so liberally. It was an earlier generation of those bright display boards, doses of instant information, quickly read and as fast forgotten.

Durlston Castle, designed by Crickmay and completed in 1888, was always a white elephant. Its latest avatar will be as Jurassic Coast Heritage Centre. So much heritage! As children, the only charm here was a model electric railway set out in a low hut. There was an aviary, too, next door to Hillcrest, out of bounds, the more interesting.

Durlston's name comes from a collapsed stone arch, 'thirl' being 'to pierce'. Its stub still stands. Durdle Door's origin is similar. The headland itself, an enclosing arm of Durlston Bay, gives rise to a considerable tidal race. The bay has eaten into many-layered Purbeck beds interspersed with clays, less resilient against an aggressive sea than massive Portland stone. Here, sheer rock is replaced by clay-rich cliff or steeply sloping thickets running down to a rocky beach. Sunnydale, a shallow valley, funnels a little stream when it rains. Another follows it underground. When BP drilled further up the dale slurry from their borehole discoloured the water in Durlston Bay. Prolonged rain regularly sets the land slipping. In 1960 Burt's Zigzag descent to the shore was damaged and the sewer broken. The following summer saw a marvellous crop of tomatoes, their seeds having passed through the folk above!

That landslide, if it taught developers nothing, gave my younger brother Charles, then at Hillcrest, a first lesson in law. A corner of the school's grounds including matron's cottage disappeared. Some tile floor is still visible. It was uninsured, he told us, because it was an 'Act of God'. He is now a lawyer. God acted, too, to threaten the foolishly-situated clifftop flats. 15th January 1983: 'Beyond the Zigzag, at the highest point of the cliff, there has been a considerable fall - bringing a new block of flats nearer its demise.' But you and I as taxpayers, not the developers or tenants, spent a huge sum shoring up the cliff to preserve an eyesore.

Purbeck stone was quarried from these cliffs, worked and manhandled onto boats below until the end of the 19th century. In 1854 the beds yielded some unique marsupial fossils. Two years later Samuel Beccles, working systematically, unearthed 27 species new to science just below the Belle Vue Café. That became a pub, as the Tilly Whim Inn famous for its strip shows. 14th July 1970: '...All I saw through the crowd of overheated youths was a blonde head and one tit!...There was a group of London boys, black and white in harmony, trying to start a riot with the locals - no one seemed prepared to pick up the challenge.' It was seriously damaged in a fire in 1972 and demolished soon afterwards.

From Hillcrest we could watch RAF target practice. One of the planes (Nick Mack, then in the class above, assures me they were Meteors) towed a zeppelin-like target over Durlston Bay whilst others attacked it. Once the target buckled and fell into the bay.

Peveril Point, sloping to the sea as the second arm embracing Durlston Bay, was an important mediaeval source of stone. How much has its profile been created by quarrying? Two burr stone ledges, the same bed showing as two sides of a syncline, run out into the waves. Below the concrete bunker and south of the northern ledge Purbeck marble, blue and full of water snails, outcrops on the shore. The marble for Canterbury Cathedral may have come from here.

With the two important stones so easily available so near to water transport, there must have been large scale quarrying here, perhaps even a jetty. Today, Peveril Point's main significance is as the southern breakwater sheltering Swanage Bay, once the harbour of the largest town in Purbeck.

SWANAGE: PORT TO RESORT

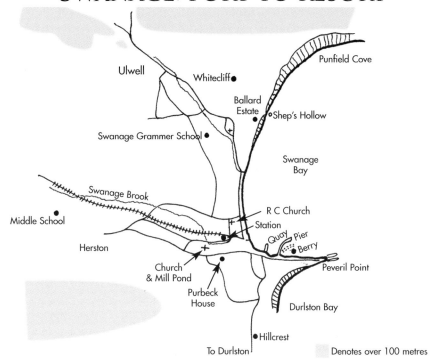

Ulwell
Whitecliff●
Punfield Cove
Ballard
Estate
● ●Shep's Hollow
Swanage Grammer School ●
Swanage
Bay
Swanage Brook
Middle School ●
R C Church
Station
Herston
Quay Pier
●Berry
Church
& Mill Pond
Peveril Point
Purbeck
House
Durlston Bay
●Hillcrest
To Durlston
Denotes over 100 metres

The name of Swanage has not travelled far from the 'Swanawic' of 9th century documents. Was it derived from swans or swine? Perhaps the beach trapped the river in a lagoon as at Weymouth. Swans would have liked that. So would W.M. Hardy, who postulates an ancient waterway navigable by small boats as far as Herston. Builders like him, with practical experience of what remains underground, are better sources than those who theorise above it.

A battery on Peveril Point, complete with cannon, guarded the little port until the close of the 19th century. Beneath it the north shore of the point passes the lifeboat slip, the fishermen's slipway and the clockless clock-tower, a memorial to the Duke of Wellington never intended to preside over this seaside view. All three are late 19th century. The lifeboat came in 1875. To make way for the construction of the Old Pier and its tramway, the fishermen were shifted here from their old haunt east of the stone quay.

There, a permanent freshwater spring still bubbles up generously at Monkey Beach, so-called because 'monkey boats' from ocean-going vessels would land here, sailors filling barrels to replenish their water supply. As for the clock-tower, it was part of George Burt's *objets trouvé*. The pier created a new curve of beach, Buck Shore where the Sailing Club is now based. We had a dinghy there as kids and soon learned to avoid a nasty rock, the Berry, which emerges at low tide below the clock-tower. The burr outcrops not far away and I always thought the Berry a rock *in situ*. In fact it is the highest point of a forgotten breakwater made of blocks of marble and burr. Who built it when? It was well-established in 1858 when Brannon mentions a plan for the first pier to '...cross the Berry Rock' but it is unlikely to be a survival from a mediaeval pier.

Swanage thrived modestly as a fishing village in the sheltered southwest corner of the bay at the mouth of a tiny river. The bay changed little over the centuries: the white headland of Ballard, clay cliffs reducing southwards to the estuary of the brook then coming to closure with Peveril Point. Man has fundamentally altered the detail.

The town expanded from the 17th century, when demand for paving and tile soared after the 1666 Fire of London. Then, most Purbeck stone quarries fell within the parish, the worked stone leaving from Swanage beach. Until 1861 when the utilitarian first pier was completed, there was only the 1780 stone jetty. Even afterwards, given fine weather, horses dragged great-wheeled carts of stone goods through the water to rowed barges which served 'stonehackers', sea-going sailing vessels. William Craft's wonderful 'naïve' 1869 painting beautifully records that period, showing the stone quay, carts, rowing boats being loaded and glorious sailing vessels.

Stone merchants stacked goods for shipment along the seaside east of Institute Road and north of the High Street. Much was unfinished, so the place echoed with the sound of hammer against chisel or punch. The 'Bankers' where the stonecutters worked stood amongst 'stacks of stone on raised platforms intersected by wagon roads' and gave the name to the whole. A tramway from the pier was to carry stone from Langton and Durlston Bay, coal and fish to and from a depot west of the quay. The line still runs to that depot, familiar to us as the amusement arcade, Playland. In that incarnation it housed many gaming machines where, for the big, old penny, you could try your luck. Some, shaken at a crucial stage, disgorged their pennies generously.

A print dated 1856 in later editions of Brannon's book shows the pier and a steam engine plying the line before either existed. The steam engine never did arrive. In the first edition of 1858 neither features. They were neatly added to the plate later, leaving the date unchanged.

Marine Villas, now at the base of the pier but then on unblemished seaside, was an opening salvo in a battle to transform Swanage. Built by William Morton Pitt in 1825, it had a billiard room, café and baths for well-to-do visitors. Earlier he had adapted the manor house as a genteel hotel. It became The Victoria after the princess's stay in 1833. In the 1950s, both the Victoria and Grosvenor hotels were owned by a Colonel Balls. In the backstreet, behind 'the Vic', he had a piggery which was run by one 'Piggy' Crabbe. For the well-to-do, tourism was the future and The Bankers a major bone of contention. Sir Charles Robinson, retired from London, was their most vocal opponent. He had a grievance against quarries: his first house in Park Road collapsed into an underground in 1873. His son agreed in 1882 that The Bankers stood '...where there should be gravel-strewn gardens...more hostile to Swanage as a great watering place than the narrow, inconvenient streets.' Great stone carts dropping mud and slurry blocked the High Street and The Bankers obscured the view. Startling arrogance earned Sir Charles the title Taty Greens after he pulled up potato plants beside a quarry and threw them down the shaft in a protest against quarrying on his newly-acquired land. In 1875 a charge against a quarryman for shouting 'Taty Greens' at his son was dismissed and young Robinson was fined £1 for striking him with a stick. But the Swanage establishment and the landowners had become rich, articulate incomers. Against them the quarrymen and the stone merchants were on a losing wicket. The arrival of the railway in 1885 defused the situation. Independent of weather, rail became the principal mode of transport, serving a new stone yard at the bottom of Court Hill. One last celebrated dispute over a quarryman's right to dig an underground anywhere resulted in 'Bosser' Lander being sent to jail in 1903 for contempt of court. The Bankers faded as men abandoned quarries at Durlston Bay and above Swanage in favour of Bankes Estate lands around Langton.

Two Swanage men, John Mowlem (1788-1868) and his nephew, George Burt (1816-94), contractors with fortunes made in London, both returned to transform the town. Mowlem built improving structures including the Mowlem Institute (1863), an unlovely nonconformist chapel to self-improvement set beside the river mouth, ancestor to an equally unlovely successor (1967). Near it he commemorated a great but fanciful naval victory over the Danes in 877 with a granite pillar incongruously capped with cannon balls. In fact, the Danish ships were wrecked. But Danish craft came later: I remember one with a striped red and white sail crossing the bay in 1949. I was six, as was Tom Wollen of St George's School when he saw one high and dry at Pegwell Bay in Kent. They proved to be the same. His mother, Caroline, tells me that the *Hugin* (named after one of Thor's ravens) was rowed across from Denmark in 1949 to commemorate the landing of Hengist and Horsa in 449. Its visit to Swanage seems to have been part of a newspaper publicity stunt.

Mowlem's obelisk to Prince Albert's 1862 visit, inscribed simply 'Albert the Good' was taken down between the wars. The plinth remained until 1971 when, to a brief furore, a developer demolished and dumped it. Trev, taking pity, stored it at St Aldhelm's Quarry where it waits recall as 'heritage'.

'King of Swanage', Burt built castelled Purbeck House in the High Street. It became the convent, my first school, then a hotel. He brought in piped water, half the lost monuments in London and set Swanage climbing the hill towards Durlston. At the bottom of Park Road his single storey market has since gained two floors, but retains fine carved key-stones: a bull, hares, a pair of fish, fruit.... Next to it he put up a waterworks in 1864 but it is his Water Tower of 1886 that dominates the hilltop skyline. Robert and I used to shoot feral pigeons in it for the owner, then pass them on to Paddy Birkill for emergency supplies in Oldfeld - 'Olditz' - the boarding part of the Grammar School.

In 1905 the seafront was sheathed in a raised stone promenade, a signal victory of tourism over industry. Swanage was spreading northwards, too, as red brick villas. Timber groynes were added to trap sand.

According to Robinson, the first pier was '... a rough, shambling timber jetty with nets, lobster pots and fishermen around it. Stonehackers load there and coal is delivered.' Paddle steamers carrying trippers from Bournemouth brought popular tourism, running along the coast, even across to France. Their popularity soon warranted another, smarter pier (1897), still flourishing in my boyhood. In summer the paddle steamers *Embassy, Consul, Empress of India*, each with its single yellow and black funnel (*Monarch* had two) plied to Bournemouth, the Isle of Wight and Weymouth. Their rivals were copper-green demobbed war-time patrol boats *Dunkirk, Anzio* and *Matapan*. We rarely went on the paddle steamers. An Isle of Wight trip in the late 40s was aborted halfway back (we got off at Bournemouth) when I was sick into my sunhat. My father hurled it into the ship's wake. White, that hat was, with thin navy and orange bands around its neck, against my brother's plain white one. How could I forget or forgive? My brother, not I, mourned each steamer's passing, writing to the company in 1950 when *Monarch* was scrapped. They sent him a large, battered pennant, 'Monarch' printed along it in white tape. Since regular steamer runs ceased in 1966 there is only the *Waverley's* annual visit.

We fished off the pier, catching smelt, pollack, pout whiting but mostly 'bunners' - rough wrasse. Once I hooked a fishing rod but someone, certainly not the loser, claimed it and gave me five bob. It was worth much more! Both piers were cut off at the base as a wartime precaution. The New Pier's link was restored. The Old Pier remained isolated but we boys could still make our way out over splinter-ridden timbers to its tip. The near section, boarded over and with diving boards facing the New Pier, was held by the Swimming Club. During a nightmare competition and in front of many admirers, a graceful dive took my trunks. I regained them to loud, humiliating applause. The New Pier's decline was checked after 1992 when Purbeck District Council bought it from developers for one pound. Many people donated towards its repair and today it serves as a promenade and a stand for anglers.

One of my grandmothers lived south of the chalk ridge in Swanage, the other south of the same ridge in Freshwater, Isle of Wight. My parents met in India at a party given by Sir Theodore Tasker, who coincidentally retired to Swanage from a distinguished career in the Indian Civil Service. He once told me how he had been sent with two other officials to persuade the miserly, but immensely rich Nizam of Hyderabad to finance improvements in his state. In a grassed courtyard they found several wooden chariots laden with silver bullion sunk to their axles. To delay them, the Nizam insisted they communicate with him in Persian. He rose to join the Viceroy's Council before descending to become a governor at the Grammar School where, such a distant figure, we knew him as Theobald.

My father first came to Swanage when working in the War Office: '...to see the Welsh Division's Battle School...at Oldfeld (Harrow House)...Your mother and I spent a week in June '42 at the Ship Hotel - there was scaffolding along the shore but it didn't prevent your mother swimming.' So I was conceived in the Ship (where a bomb killed five two months later), opposite the appropriately-named Lower Pleasure Gardens which until recently housed subterranean public lavatories. These, along with the vanished ones on Court Hill, were recycled air-raid shelters. The 'Troc', also opposite, in peace a refined restaurant, housed the forces canteen, patronised by RAF personnel then American troops. They had the first floor whilst, according to my aunt the baker's downstairs sold the sawdust cakes and grey bread of wartime. Concrete 'dragon's teeth' ran the length of the seafront and below the tide line that scaffolding.

Geoff Hooper, as a little boy, saw a man demonstrating a new kind of fire escape by jumping out of the turret of the building on the corner between Station Road and Institute Road. Older, a showing of *Snow White* which he had just seen at the cinema was outclassed when a Messerschmitt flew over low trailing black smoke. It crashed near Afflington and later he went to see it.

I crossed and recrossed the seafront, splendid in a basketwork seat on the back of my mother's bicycle. She would lean the bike against a patch of brick next to Boots (still unaltered) and I descended for another shopping expedition. The 'dragons teeth', faint memory, were demolished in the late forties save a few that survived for years near the Mowlem. To our delight, a steamroller renewing the pavement fell over the seafront and sat some weeks half on, half off. The 'scaffolding' retreated northwards, rusting to oblivion at

Punfield Cove where joints still lie. A sign 'Danger! Mines! Keep Out!' stood near the Ocean Bay and 'things' would appear on the beach. One spat satisfying flame when we kicked it. We were luckier than five school-boys killed near Shep's Hollow in 1955 while trying to open a landmine with a shoe-horn. Kids are harsh. Hearing the blast in class, we went to admire the hole in the beach afterwards. Playing with munitions, not stepping on them, caused all those post-war accidents. They warned us of strange things, not strange people. Without 'stranger danger' slogans to darken our days we learned street-wisdom as kids should. Adults were generally helpful and supportive, often informative, sometimes fierce on scrumpers and trespassers, a tiny handful too physically affectionate.

We were launched at five, going alone by bus to the convent. The main hazard was the Bashing-up Boys who lurked occasionally just off Spring Hill. We were sweet little kids in bright blue blazers. The Bashing-up Boys, led by Booby Slagger, weren't sweet nor did they wear blazers. Who was Booby Slagger? He certainly existed, but under what name? There was 'Beardie', too, familiar to all my generation. Not old, perhaps not forty, he walked Swanage in a dirty mackintosh, sometimes shouted. He was scarey, not dangerous. Some said he was a naval officer crossed in love. Perhaps a superficial resemblance to the sailor on the Player's cigarette packet made him such.

Later, we changed buses at the Mowlem for Hillcrest. While waiting outside the Mowlem for the Durlston service we would climb down the cast iron pipes (now gone) to explore. We dug tiny eels and flatfish from the sandy bed of the stream or advanced under the bridge, prominently dated 1910, and up the big pipe that so-insultingly confines the brook. It soon got very dark. None of us braved it to the far end. Further upstream, by the church we caught eels and sticklebacks using our mothers' stockings. Then, with a secondhand cycle, I grew out of buses. We were gamblers, too, setting dares and using sweets for counters. I won a 6d ice cream for towing a raw sprat the length of the seafront behind my bike then eating it. It may not have cleared the taste, but it was good for my street cred!

Our house was close to Swanage Grammar School, then at its peak. The school divided into four houses, each named for a Purbeck headland – Ballard, Peveril, Durlston and St Aldhelm's. As well as competing in various sports and debates there was an annual Festival, taking in music, singing, acting, painting and creative writing. Siblings remained together, so my brothers, sister and I were all in St Aldhelm's.

Anthony, my elder brother, tried to pull a trump: if he didn't get more pocket money he'd do a paper-round. Gambling on parental disapproval he lost, so we all ended up doing paper-rounds. A hard way to earn ten bob (50 pence) a week, it meant early rising and cycling a heavy trade bike across the seafront, whatever the weather, hands grey with printer's ink. Rarely, when

The stone carrying vessel 'The Ripple';
a cross-section of Swanage rock

a high spring tide coincided with an easterly gale, the waves washed over the seafront, leaving sand and weed behind. Then we took De Moulham Road, roughly metalled with white chalk as were many New Swanage roads. One day the 6.30 news announced that the Russians had put a satellite into orbit, that the 'bleep, bleep' they broadcast came from *Sputnik*, a manmade grapefruit in Space. It seemed incredible.

We saw things in the early morning. Not just Miss Malpus, who ran the tiny shop beyond Whitecliff Crossroads, walking though the snow for her daily bathe. There might be a great ship at anchor or a passing submarine. Sometimes there were porpoises close in around the groynes. Unusual birds appeared. A raven commuting between its nest on Ballard and Durlston Bay led us to a dolphin's corpse. There were wild geese in winter, oiled birds chilling to death on the sand. Seasonal events included the first wheatear or swallow, then the last. One morning I rescued a tiny leveret from a cat, raised it to full size until it was banished after pissing on my grandmother's knee. We released it at St Aldhelm's Head. Things washed up - boats, corpses, big fish. Unseasonal easterlies regularly wrecked beach huts or, more rarely, swan-shaped pedaloes. We pushed a hand-cart from Hill & Churchills (now Martin's) to the Station to collect the papers off the early train. Who first noticed the hole in the window of Rose's the Jewellers in Station Road? A real robbery!

Almost everyone at school had some religious allegiance, practised or unpractised. The Church of England kids, safely superior, were most lax. Jews, the only non-Christians, too few to fit into the Universal Plan, warranted neither positive nor negative attention. We were Catholics, my father Anglican. Richard Dunham, my best friend at Hillcrest, was Plymouth Brethren. Not that we spoke of it. We accepted the evils of religion unquestioningly, never blaming them on an omnipotent god. Oddly, Richard's mother and mine got on well, perhaps each wise enough to find ungodly the more-extreme strictures of her inherited faith.

I only entered two other churches, St Aldhelm's Chapel (demolished in 1972) in Grosvenor Road for such innocuous rituals as the school carol service, and unfinished All Saints in Ulwell Road where we climbed amongst the scaffolding after the builders had gone home. Other kids were almost as parochial. None of Swanage's churches is outstanding. The parish church might have had a character of its own before the Victorians standardised it in 1859. Now the 13th century tower alone is original.

As an altar boy I wore a cassock (red or black according to religious season) and white laced cotta, held the brass 'boat' full of incense whilst my brother swayed the thurible. We chanted the responses in Latin, even understood a word or two. When commanded, we went to confession but didn't disturb the priest with real sins. The last time I entered the Catholic church was in 1975 when Trev and I removed the 'Whore of Babylon' some lost soul had scratched across the altar. It is unremarkable save for a large triptych painted by Francis Newbery in 1927 showing a youthful and innocent Edward the Martyr between St Aldhelm holding Sherborne Abbey and St Elgiva, Abbess of Shaftesbury.

Newbery took his faces from local people. Most are forgotten, but Helen Muspratt features amongst the angels. She and her sister, Joan, gifted photographers, were encouraged by the Newberys. Between the wars, as Helen Dunman, she became a leading British portraitist. Joan stayed in Swanage, running a studio in Institute Road. (The painter, Dennis Lowson, has it now). Rather fey, nervous, she took our family portraits and we mimicked her surreptitiously. She would say, 'Watch the birdie....Taken!' A bomb hit that block in 1942. Eight died in the neighbouring bank. The Muspratts were unhurt but their negatives were destroyed.

As we grew so did the world, extending from our garden to those family walks we christened 'wetties'. Often we were taken on Ballard Down, past walled Whitecliff Farm, said to be one of King John's hunting lodges. Certainly Paul Nash, the painter, had lived there in 1934. Then we set off alone, bird nesting in Spring, towards the beach in summer to swim, to play in Nutwood, a favourite thicket, or fire arrows at a rival gang across Shep's Hollow. In autumn we'd dam the stream and play 'Dam-Busters' with the more sturdy fireworks of the time. In a nearby derelict bungalow, Wentworth, our haunted house, I accidentally locked myself inside a cupboard, a few minutes of never-forgotten claustrophobia. Sometimes we crunched along the shingle to Punfield Cove, to climb up onto the grass above Paddlebox to heat a tin of beans over a fire. Around 1970, when people, not trusts, owned much of Purbeck, Dick was allowed a shack there, his home on and off ever since. When they took over, The National Trust tried unsuccessfully to evict him. Nearby, a path (lost now) led up the angle of the cliff and along the foot of the hill.

Most old accounts of Swanage mention handsome elms. Those along the foot of Ballard Down were among the finest. Another row separated Journey's End field from a lovely little meadow, now a tarmac car park. Its spring was never quite subdued. Those elms held the rookery, 36 nests in 1957, an annual challenge to climb into the swaying slender, high branches to pinch an egg from each nest. I remember one that broke in my mouth, spitting the bloody life down through the branches. That cured me. Dutch Elm disease, arriving in Purbeck in the mid seventies, cleared all those elms.

On rainy days there were books and the radio. Like so many, my first television experience was the coronation, the Misses Cook next door having one of Swanage's few sets. There was no Punch and Judy show when I was little. That came later, causing a furore in 1990–91. Peter and Wendy, who put on the show, were asked at short notice to move aside for one day for a council-organised army commando display. Wendy decided to turn this into a political issue, putting up an anti-military banner. The council, hitherto very reasonable with them, reacted by banning Punch and Judy. A sinister sideline quite deflected attention from the original dispute: the crocodile in the show had been observed eating Mrs Thatcher. Obviously there was too much red in that striped kiosk. Scandalised, half the council was prepared to maintain the ban, only the mayor's casting vote restored sanity.

In early Grammar School days my friends were Robert Smith, then living in Ballard Estate, and Richard Verge, still at Ulwell Farm. Robert's grandfather could recall cutting wheat by hand on the site of the Grand Hotel. Richard's place, with barns and a large garden, had the edge over either of ours. In its outhouses we kept oiled seabirds in 1957, each earning an RSPCA medal of doubtful gold. Later, the Miss Cooks surrendered rusty tins of pilchards, wartime emergency rations, to an injured young gull I had raised. It stayed loose in our garden for 18 months until, chased by a dog, it found it could fly and left. A week later when cycling along the seafront to collect my newspapers I saw a flock of gulls and made the feeding call I had used for mine. It detached itself, swam in and I carried it home. When it finally flew off a little later I knew it could cope.

At Ulwell Farm we experimented successfully, but not lethally, with gunpowder. We had air-guns, too. Robert still has a crooked finger from trying to rescue the target and as a large, loved goldfish floated to the surface I learned that, when shooting through water you should aim to hit if you want to miss. The Verges had television. Each Tuesday night I cycled up narrow, winding Ulwell Road for 'Quatermass and the Pit' and raced home in terror afterwards. I would have been even more nervous had I known the farm stood on the edge of an ancient graveyard used until the 7th century. We helped excavate it in 1982, turning up the only grave object, a piece of rusty metal, perhaps a knife, at the waist of one skeleton.

The stream at Ulwell was open in the 1950s, rippling over gravel alongside the road, disappearing underground only to cross beneath it. It went on to flow behind our house and was prone to flooding, as were the drains, spreading sewage across the garden. Towards the end of WWI, Mary remembers passing through Ulwell in their American buggy and seeing a row of soldiers watering horses at it. There was a POW camp there until 1919, one hut surviving long into my time as a bungalow, another as Ulwell's chapel. The stream left the road behind Mill Cottages which bear two dates. '1694' relates to the romantic old mill, '1896' to its replacement by the present cottages. That decayed mill was a popular picturesque subject for Victorian painters and photographers.

In the last years at school we began to visit the pubs, each starting, for honour's sake, underage. Hard for me, since I looked it. At first the Purbeck was favourite, then a pokey little pub of small bars. It was the hangout of a slightly 'beat' arty set rather older than ourselves, including Padraig Macmiadhachain, who proved the most successful. Currently he favours bright primitive landscapes, often views of St Aldhelm's Head. When the Purbeck's popularity waned fashion shifted to other pubs up and down the High Street. Often working or travelling away, I usually returned in summer, sometimes joining the staff of the Grosvenor Hotel as a waiter. It drew young people from far afield, some of whom settled. The men lived along a corridor fondly known as Death Row. Entertainment was not far off. The Victoria, with its popular Shades bar, was owned by Peter Sutherland, who employed the best-looking youths. He benignly looked the other way as they fleeced him. In the back of the building was a coffee bar, known as Peter's Hole. Later it was eclipsed by another with a juke box, The Bizarre, in a vanished jerry-built place in Town Hall Lane. The Grosvenor integrated The Grove(1838), probably the earliest of the Victorian villas which were to be Swanage's future. The old town, with its cramped High St, was doomed.

The late 19th century saw transformation everywhere in Swanage. "...The spectacle of the back of the High St from the banks of the stream midway, where is the queerest jumble of gables and chimneys, projecting and retreating housewalls, outhouses, garden fences and trees" of Robinson's day gave way to orderly houses as most of these were destroyed. The untamed brook was driven underground to appear cosmetically and high-walled beside the Parish Church, old Rectory and Conservative Club. It still protests with periodic flooding, 'solved' by projects which, as the inhabitants of Eldon Terrace will confirm, never quite work. The most recent multi-million pound scheme created a new jetty in 1993 at the centre of the bay. In September 2002 I watched Eldon Terrace flood again!

George Burt demolished cottages by the High St to accommodate the Restoration façade of the Mercer's Hall he had brought from London for the Town Hall. Those who met there demolished much of what remained. Opposite was an ancient bay-windowed antique shop run by ancient Mr Edge where we kids shopped for treasures such as old books and Victorian stamps. He had pages of Penny Reds, but Penny Blacks cost dear. The well in his garden, so he told us, was the very one into which Edward the Martyr had been hurled. We half believed him. The council flattened it in 1959 for a car-park, now replaced by flats. Virginia Cottage, next to the Town Hall, also sold old books. What the Nazis did to Wesley's Cottage the council did to Virginia Cottage. The picturesque Mill Pond, fed by a generous spring, powered a mill. Its last incarnation, built in 1754, had outlived any function so that corner was under threat. Demolition was delayed by WWII, during which the Nazis partially implemented council policy. Now it graces many postcards. Today The Narrows is only a name. As a child I remember its bombed houses and the spectacularly narrow street between pavements below the Black Swan.

Beyond The Narrows the High Street led on to end at Herston Cross. As children we could look across from Ballard Down to see the council houses going up along Greasehead, south of the valley road. In 1958 the Secondary Modern, now Middle School. rose opposite. Beyond Coombe Corner the road forks, the left branch rising onto the limestone ridge to Langton Matravers.

LANGTON:
CURRENT STONE CAPITAL

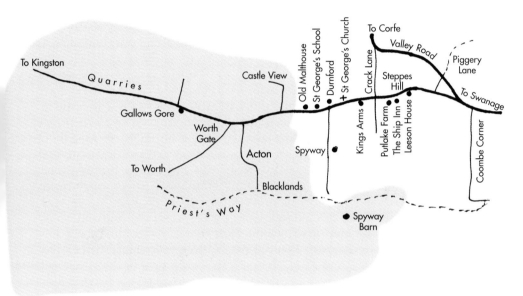

Denotes over 100 metres

The name says it: Langton is a long village. The parish ran from one estate into another. The west, Langton Wallis, once held by the Wallys family, belonged to the Bankes Estate until 1981. The east, Langton Matravers, briefly under the Maltravers of Lychett, passed to the Serrell family and Encombe Estate. Old Mrs Serrell, who died in 1884, should have stood as an uniting figure, for she was a Bankes, thus a 'westerner' by birth and an eastern Serrell by marriage. Sly Mrs Panton doesn't miss her out '...a most extraordinary woman who spent her money lavishly, and kept the villagers amused by a good band and many other entertainments got up at her own cost. True, she emptied the church, for, having the usual feud on with the parson, her band played gaily during service time...'

The east of the village dominant, 'Langton Matravers' is used for the whole village, which sprawls along the Kingston road, turnpiked in 1761 as the main route from Swanage to Corfe. Pedestrian steps up from Putlake Farm created Steppeshill. After the mid-19th century much traffic from Corfe followed the valley route but turned up Three Acre Lane to Leeson Gate before descending into Herston.

For me Langton barely featured until I was thirteen. That spring I cycled up there several times to look at cliff birds, see the cannon at Hedbury. After Trev and I became friends it grew very familiar. The ascent from Swanage was tough, especially on a heavy, gearless trade-bike. Usually we started out from his place in Gypshayes, heading for the cliffs or the valley woods. The village hasn't changed radically. At one point there were four shops. Prior's with the post office was next to The King's Arms and Ryall and Dallengers opposite, further down. Up the hill, just below North Street, David Pushman ran a tiny third shop, stocking newspapers, sweets and tobacco which gave way to a short-lived pie and chips shop in the mid 1970s. Now its a studio. The Top Shop, founded in 1842, is the oldest and highest of all the shops at the edge of the village. It was a general store in the 1920s, stocking food, hardware, shoes and quarrymen's clothes. It was owned by Mr Smith who had the draper's in Swanage. A large man with curly white hair, Mary remembers him walking to and fro each day from Swanage. No cars or gyms in those days. Walking or cycling to work was part of the day.

There was a dairy, too, White's Bakery across from the pub and, above Durnford, a garage and petrol station. Alan Marsh, living almost opposite North Street was gifted with a quirky eye, capable of turning any object into art. He died in 1997 and an exhibition of his work held in the village hall must have surprised most of its visitors by his versatility. Unsurprisingly, it moved to the Morley Gallery in London. Mary remembers his father, Oliver Marsh, combining the repair of farm tools, wheelwrighting, furniture-making, coffin-making and undertaking. His work survives in some wooden chests at Dunshay. Another of her Langton memories is of watching the smithy at his workshop round the corner forging a cart wheel's iron rim then, still red hot so that it charred the wood, fitting it.

The roof of the mediaeval church, St George's, was rebuilt in 1828, leaving it oddly higher than the squat 15th century tower. Then came radical reconstruction in 1875-76. Before the Dissolution a religious house stood at Wilkeswood, within the parish, with a chapel of St Leonard. In recognition, an aisle of the church also bears his dedication. At the corner of the churchyard, overlooking the main street, is Mary Spencer Watson's millennium commission - a figure of a mason punching a piece of stone. I like the piece. So did Geoff Hooper, a lifetime in the industry, who wrote a poem *Credit Where Overdue*:

There should have been a statue long ago
To all those men whose names we do not know
Although forgotten by posterity
They brought so many lovely things to be
Great architects without a trace of guilt
Take all the praise for everything that's built
Though quoin and jamb and mullion and arch
The columns and the fabric of the church
Are all the products of the mason's skill
Without which they would be on paper still
So thanks! At last, Miss Mary, even though
There should have been a statue long ago.

The focus of the stone industry changed over time. Most Purbeck stone quarries had been around Swanage and Durlston Bay but trouble with new landowners at the close of the 19th century encouraged men to work elsewhere. Many shifted to land of the Bankes Estate around Langton where good stone in the Middle Purbeck beds is less deeply buried. Few dug the Lower Purbeck stones lying below a thick, tough bed of useless 'cinder' made up of oyster shells. That forms the floor of most Langton diggings and marks a period of marine deposits forming the boundary between the Jurassic and Cretaceous eras.

The topmost Purbeck beds, marble and burr had long been exploited but the ones below did not become important until the early 17th century. Then, Downsvein was particularly valuable, splitting easily along the bed to produce the thin slabs required for roof tile and paving. Much was sent to London. Fiennes notes that in her day most of the houses were made of stone and that there were many quarries. Daniel Defoe, who came here in 1720 talks of '...vast quantities of stone, which is cut out flat, and used in London in great quantities for paving courtyards, alleys, avenues to houses, kitchens, footways on the sides of high streets, and the like.' Other Middle Purbeck beds such as thornback were and are exploited for ledgers and headstones. At first digging was open-cast but in the early 18th century when the most accessible stone had been worked out quarrymen began to sink mines. By the early 19th century the majority of Purbeck stone was extracted by underground mining.

Armed with shovel, pick and bar a sloping shaft was sunk to the level of the bed required - still often Downsvein. Other beds often mined were Lannen vein, freestone and New vein. Sinking a new shaft was not as intimidating as it might appear, the beds of stone being separated by considerable layers of clay and shale. Nevertheless, it required a great deal of labour. Once the desired bed was reached the quarryman advanced a 'lane' into it. This was a narrow corridor, its roof supported by 'legs'. The sloping shaft was set with flat paviers so that the stone would run up it more easily, but there were steps for men to come and go beside this 'slide'. A lifting apparatus was set up at its mouth. This consisted of a simple capstan set three metres or so from the shaft. Two long, flat 'crabstones', pierced through, set vertical in the ground and buttressed towards the shaft held a 'collar' which kept the thick wooden 'post' upright. A pole 'spack' was passed into a hole through this post cut above a metre up. This left a long end projecting, to which a donkey was harnessed. A rope (replaced by chain around 1800) attached to the post ran down the shaft to hold a small four-wheeled cart, a 'trundle'.

Underground, the men used 'paddles' to dig block free of clay and punches, wedges and bars to separate it from its neighbours. The wheels of the cart were set in from the sides, allowing it to tilt and making it easier to manoeuvre a block on board. The loaded cart was pushed to the foot of the slide and the donkey, walking round, wound the chain onto the post, raising the stone to the surface. It was a tough life, spent largely in damp darkness lit by candles, stooped in a lane often only 1.5 m high beneath the low roof and always at risk from the unstable ceiling. This method of quarrying stopped soon after WWII when ever-larger mechanical diggers made light of the overburden.

A network of unmapped tunnels warren the eastern section of the Purbeck stone ridge, their collapse causing gentle dips in the landscape. We learned about the extent of the underground network in October 1960. While Mr Haysom was opening a new quarry at Worth Gate the bulldozer broke into an old underground. Trev and I spent a wet day with a tape measure, compass and torch mapping the system. In two places the 'lane' we entered turns sharply away after knocking through into someone else's. Stone 'legs' supported the precarious ceiling, aided by the occasional black, rotted timber. There were patches of candle soot, a stub of candle and a pit of clear water beside the lane. We came across bats, which must have entered through some unblocked shaft lost in bramble thickets to sleep in the stable subterranean environment. I still have the map we made that day. In 1992 Trev broke into another underground at Landers Quarry, near the top of Haycrafts Lane. There, in the clay, was the print of a small hob-nailed boot perhaps left by an 18th century quarryman. In the ceiling were swelling 'boils' caused by the sediment of the bed above filling a dinosaur footprint in the lower bed.

In 1974 Brian Bugler (grandson of Eric Benfield, author of 'Purbeck Shop'), the brothers Freddie and Dennis Smale (co-author with Langton's David Lewer of the excellent 'Swanage Past' and Charlie Turner formed a Purbeck Stone Quarries Preservation Group. They surveyed every

A Cretateous dinosaur footprint in a slab of the roach bed of Purbeck stone; the emblem of St. George's First School, Langton Matravers

'underground' still accessible (some 30), including one beneath the flats overlooking Durlston Bay. There was a plan to open one for visitors, but the insurance proved prohibitive.

Footprints left by giant saurians are dramatic but quite common in the Purbeck beds, especially the roach. Some appear as three-toed indentations as the beast walked over wet mud, the tail leaving its own trace. It was a long time before these damaging flaws in the plane surface were recognised as footprints. Now they increase stone's value. A long trail of prints found in Suttle's Quarry in 1963 and now at the Natural History Museum in London caused a considerable stir. There was a print in the paving of the Haysoms' driveway, visible only when a shower produced a three-toed puddle.

Merchants controlled the stone trade, buying up the produce of many small family businesses and selling it on in bulk. Finished tile, kerb, paving or sinks were transported by farm cart (a nice sideline for the farmers) down to Swanage where it was shipped out. In the 1920s there was an attempt to by-pass the merchants by founding a co-operative with fixed prices. One man advised his son, Trev's father, to take no part in it, having heard the names of its organisers. Marion Harden told how her father and brother, then working in Portland, sunk all their savings into the co-op. Their mother, back in Langton, advised them to withdraw it. They didn't, and lost the price of a cottage when men broke ranks and it collapsed.

When living in Acton I was surrounded by the sound of iron against steel, the pitching and punching of stone as men turned out yards of dubbers, lintels and quoins. Only the more mechanised workshops had saws and polishers to make headstones, hearths and mantelpieces. Almost all the quarries are still worked by long-established families: Lovell, Bower, Haysom, Bonfield, Lander, Keates, Norman and the like. Today the most popular beds are Thornback, Grubb, Wetson bed, Inland Freestone and, recently Cap.

East of Afflington Barn quarries spread along the north side of the road past Gallows Gore. The name inspired unsupported rumours of swinging corpses left by Judge Jeffreys' bloody hand, slain Monmouth Rebels from 1685. Men were hanged in Wareham, their parts displayed elsewhere *pour decourager les autres* but not here. It appears as 'Callos Goure' on a 1772 map and 'gore' is an old word, in this case denoting not blood but a triangular plot of land. Across the road from the row of Gallows Gore Cottages is Lander's Quarry. Titus Lander turned up several prehistoric sites as he dug here. Mary, growing up nearby, recalls him with affection because under his tuition she learned to handle the tools that brought her to sculpture.

As a boy, Langton church's only impact was that it held Trev for choir practice one evening a week. The choirmaster was Reg Saville, who has since thrown light on much of the history of the village and played a major role in establishing the museum behind the church. This focuses largely on the stone industry.

The King's Arms, opposite the church, opened as The Mason's Arms in 1743 but Reg Saville suggests that the name was changed during a wave of patriotic fervour in the early 19th century. It was bought from the brewers by Darrell Elford in 1993, then passed to Steve Robson in 1996. His brother currently runs it as a popular free house with a reputation for good food. However, it went through a period of notoriety in the 1920s. Another pub, The Ship on Steppeshill, was rebuilt next door to the original building after a landlord's suicide in the early 1880s.

Opposite The Ship is Manor Farm, where a wooden granary stood on toadstool-like staddle stones, designed to fend off rats. The Langton Preservation Society, specially Dave Burt and John Dean, tried to save it but eventually, around 1980, it was demolished. Below the farm towards Swanage Mary Haysom's cottage was damaged by subsidence when Serrell's Mead was altered. While the problem was being solved she lent it to me. I was there when the Great Gale of October 1987 struck, waking in the small hours as the stone building shuddered. I remembered my pyjamas on the washing line. Bed was warm, the garden cold so I left them. In the morning trees, branches and wires were down, the next door apple tree lay in my garden. The pyjamas hung calmly on the line!

When we were boys, the policeman living in Gypshayes was interested in wild life, sympathetic with our attempts to curb egg-collecting. Once, seeing an egg-collector park at Spyway Barn Farm, we watched from a distance as he climbed down to a peregrine eyrie east of Dancing Ledge. Hoping to catch him red-handed, we ran back to Langton to alert P.C. Short. He was out. As we stood beside Drove the car slowly passed and his companion wound down his window to say, 'You boys should be doing your homework.'

Most Langton kids passed through St George's School, its catchment area taking in little Acton and school-less Worth. Each year it dragged a number of kids through the injustice of the 11+ exam into Swanage Grammar School. It was a cruel cut-off. Once failed, few kids crossed the bridge from Secondary Modern to Grammar School. Those that did went straight to the top of the class. St George's still flourishes on an excellent reputation and parents compete to get their kids in through its narrow doors.

Between the wars there were nine schools in the parish, mostly boys' preparatory schools. Parents posted across the Empire approved of the accessible but beautiful environment. But the Empire was slipping away. The fifties saw the twilight of the preparatory school era. Leeson House, the vicarage during the 19th century, became the school for young ladies in 1899, to which Mary used to ride her pony. Later it was opened as a boy's prep school, then was bought by the county council as a Field Studies Centre. There was an incestuous touch to some of Langton's schools. Durnford, once seat of the Serrells, was opened as a prep school by Thomas Pellatt in 1893 then closed with the 1939 war. Demolished in 1952, it was partially rebuilt as a private house retaining '1725' above its door. Pellatt married one daughter of Revd John Thomas, Chaplain and Bursar of Malborough School. Reginald Corbett married the other daughter and founded The Old Malthouse (1906), the only surviving prep school in Purbeck. Spyway school, built by Pellatt for his son-in-law, opened in the late 1930s then passed to two Warner brothers. It closed in 1976 after one brother died. Later it reopened to provide English education to teenage children of rich foreigners. The many Iranians caused concern amongst local youths because girls found them exotic, even tall, dark and handsome, always well-oiled. The fall of the Shah's regime saw a drastic decline in custom. Spyway transformed into a rehabilitation centre for problem kids. If Langton was doubtful about foreigners it was frankly hostile to this wave of occupants. They were a long way from the sweet little treble boys in caps and blazers who, for half a century, had typified outsiders. Inevitably there were problems, cars stolen, windows broken. They moved on and the place fell vacant. Sean Keeley, working on its conversion into time-share apartments, discovered a cane some boy had pushed through into the damp course. It split while we hotly debated who should try it out on whom.

Beyond Spyway is Spyway Barn Farm, notable in the fifties for its massive, recently retired cart horses. Small at the time, I remember them as slightly intimidating and probably several feet taller than they actually were. East of the farm across several fields is Cuckoo Pound, an improbable little copse blown into shape by its exposure to the prevailing southwesterlies.

The weather is different up on the ridge, fog lying thicker here and bringing confusion even amongst such small, familiar walled fields. West of Eastington the Priest's Way launches out into an open field. There, walking home late, I occasionally took several involuntary circuits before hitting something recognisable. Acton was Bedstead Country, a number of its fences patched with bits of metal bed. A boundary integrating a bedstead suggested you were near Acton.

I lived in Acton, too, having returned from India to find Trev negotiating to lease Ivy Cottage from the Bankes Estate. He didn't want to live there, merely to do it up against the future, to get his foot in the property door. He suggested I move in and together we'd do bits of work on the place. It had no electricity, a tap in the garden and an elsan down the garden path. No doubt Ivy Cottage was undermined by quarries too but I was grateful for a roof. Several weeks later Trev mentioned that, on his solicitor's advice, he had not signed the lease. Already it was home with its cast-iron fireplace, a still-functioning bread-oven sunk into the wall, and a great brass bedstead upstairs. My old Tilley lamp dripped paraffin slowly, noisily into a tin below. There was an injured kestrel for company but an orphaned baby fox escaped to certain death through a rotted gap under the door. It was a nice place to be, the garden an overgrown wilderness of buddleia and bramble. Amongst the detritus of the last inhabitant were wartime ration books and a 'Parkers' Stores' calendar celebrating the coronation of George VI. The act of crowning drifts from a radio in a waft of miasma. The Bankes Estate sometimes ran on a system of benevolent neglect. No one questioned my presence. I left a year later, setting off for India on that ill-fated motorcycle.

Mains water came late to Acton. Many cottages retained a shallow well flush with the ground and covered by a stone slab. At a party someone left the cover off. A girl, stepping back, disappeared from amongst us with a muffled splash. Lucky to miss the sides, she was hauled out, the star of the evening.

Langton parish extends north to the foot of the chalk ridge. Descending from the limestone plateau it quits the area where fields are outlined by dry stone walls for that of hedges and fences. Taking in ancient Wilkeswood, it crosses the Swanage brook. The brook's drainage system, together with that of the tributaries of the Corfe river have cut into the soft clays overlying the limestone to form the eastern section of Purbeck's central valley.

UP THE VALLEY TO CORFE

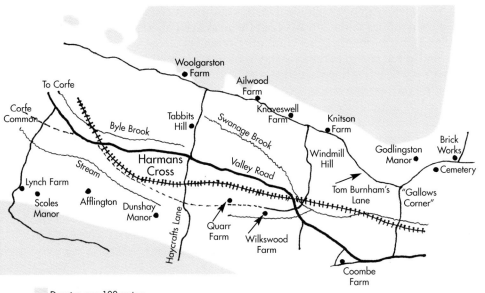

Denotes over 100 metres

A network of streamlets cut through soft Wealden clays to form the valley from Swanage to Worbarrow Bay. East of Corfe, Haycrafts Lane and Tabbits Hill mark the watershed. On the east the main brook flows towards Swanage Bay, swollen along its length by springs rising from the flanks of the valley. On the west water heads for two tributaries of Corfe River. A little ridge of hard grit carries the Valley Road and divides the flow into the western branch from that into the eastern branch. Independently, both tributaries severed the chalk ridge, isolating Corfe Castle's mound. Beyond the gap they combine. Most writers call the east stream 'Byle', the west 'Wicken', but the only name of the rivers I have heard in speech is 'Corfe'.

Three roads link Swanage to Corfe along the valley. Quiet, though undulating, the underhill Knitson road passing through a series of farms was a favourite cycle ride for us kids. Our goal was the bakery in Corfe which, we were convinced, produced unrivalled chocolate éclairs. Turning west off

Darky Lane opposite Swanage Farm it skirts the Brickworks, exploiting a seam of clay dug since the 17th century. Beyond, set back from the road, is Godlingston Manor Farm, named for a Saxon owner, Godling. Partly 13th century, it narrowly escaped demolition after a fire in 1871.

Seeing that road only in daylight, we were unaware of its potential horrors. Even my mother, not prone to superstition, said Godlingston was haunted. There was talk of a Cistercian monastery and an ethereal black monk. The modern cemetery a few hundred metres to the east enhanced the frisson. The seat of terror lies to the south, where the road from Herston meets the stretch called Tom Burnham's Lane. Until the late sixties there was a triangular grass mound at the centre of this crossing. Each lane running into it was lined with elms, so when one approached the mound the elms produced the effect of light following from behind. At the crossroads stood a dead white oak. It was my quickest route home from Langton and, if I disliked it by daylight, it took courage to go that way by night. February 1961: 'I went back in the dusk via Gallows Corner after picking up a thick stick - I kept thinking there was a light behind me. I am not very superstitious except there... Whatever happened there it's very sinister and gruesome - I've never been that way in dusk or dark and have no wish to again.' Apparently even horses dislike it. If fact is at odds with rumour, rumour is richer. I always thought Tom Burnham hanged himself from that white oak in the 1790s, and lay buried under the grassy mound because crossroads confuse the werewolves. A stake was said to have been driven through his heart. In fact he hanged himself in a nearby copse, but he was buried there.

When I was twenty and working on Brownsea Island, the magic of the place was first broken for me. I had taken an evening off to attend a party at Dunshay. My father had dropped me at the house, smart in his old dinner jacket and bow tie. The house seemed quiet and it transpired that a family crisis had swept the party aside. I was the only guest in ignorance due to being phoneless at home on Brownsea. I was offered a lift home but, embarrassed by the whole situation, I swept the offer aside and set off to walk home in thin-soled patent leather dancing shoes. Angry and frustrated, I barely noticed Tom Burnham as I passed the old oak. Since then he has been tame, but I still dislike that crossroads.

The road rises to a sharp bend on the skirts of Windmill Hill, which is situated on another lens of hard grit. Even a map dated 1765 labels it 'site of old mill'. There is nothing now but ruined Windmill Barn. There was another vanished windmill which stood on the hillock north of Coombe, where the road to Langton quits the Valley Road.

In the late fifties and sixties Kitchie Cottage at Knitson was a landmark. Kato Havas, a violinist of Hungarian origin (Kitchie being 'small' in Hungarian), lived there with her three daughters, contemporaries of ours.

There she held her summer school, and, with Sir Arthur Bliss, she set up a remarkable Purbeck Music Festival in 1954, bringing chamber music to Purbeck with concerts at local churches. It stopped abruptly when she gave up the cottate in the early 1970s. She revisited Purbeck recently but avoided Kitchie Cottage. Too many memories.

At Knaveswell the road does a switchback down to a spring and up again to Ailwood Farm. The wood is to its south. Little Woolgarston, just off the road, had been home to the distinguished singers Norman Notley and David Brynley who, from 1933 to 1953, were best known as a duo. It was a romantic association. In 1924 Notley became baritone in the celebrated English Singers, a sextet of unaccompanied voices. Brynley, who was orphaned at the age of nine, fended for himself and did a spell 'down the pit' in his Welsh village. At sixteen his voice attracted attention and led him to a number of roles in London. Later he began broadcasting for children. The men met in 1922 and lived together until Notley died in Corfe in 1980, with Brynley following nine months later.

To us the valley meant the woods, even though they comprise a small area amongst the rolling meadows. Most were private but being quicker, and with sharper senses, we managed to avoid authority. These woods were another spring haunt, where we searched for sparrowhawks' nests amongst the oaks, and those of small birds at the edges where trees descended into the thicket. In broad daylight young foxes, not yet shy, would look up in curiosity. If alone I liked to climb a spring green tree and just sit still, back to the trunk on some broad bough. Everything fled at my disturbance, but after a few minutes life resumed: birds feeding through the branches, a pied woodpecker landing on a nearby trunk. Nestlings started to beg again and parents resumed their food-bearing business. Below, russet roe deer might walk by, alert though never looking up. But what to do when a young couple chose the shelter of that tree for a row, and then, spent interminable time saying soppy things just below? They kept me from my supper.

The main highway out of Swanage, turnpiked in 1761, rose through Langton and Kingston. In the late 19th century it began to be superseded by the chalk track through the valley. In 1926 Mary remembers the friendly workmen gradually advancing from Corfe as they widened and surfaced the Valley Road. Usually she used to ride to Leeson school along the bridleway, which is known as Lynchet beyond Quarr. When that was too muddy she took the Valley Road, raised for much of its length on that undulation in the valley floor. It was marked by no major settlement. Harmans Cross grew up later, granting immortality to Harman, who lies at the intersection, they say, after hanging himself in nearby woods. The name is old, featuring on a map dated 1772.

Gerard described the valley as '...affordeing excellent Pasture for Sheepe and Feedeings for other Cattel, plentie of good Corne, alsoe Quarries of lasting Stone, and mines of spotted and blewe Marbill.' It was that marble, not the fecundity, that made this one of the busiest industrial centres in 13th century England. It runs west from Peveril Point, outcropping along the south flank of the valley and thinning westwards to a mean deposit in Worbarrow Tout and at Lulworth. Beyond Blashenwell it soon became unviable.

There are several layers, greenish or blue, but rarely red, sandwiched between thick beds of dark shales and clays. True marble is metamorphosed by heat and pressure. Purbeck marble is no marble, merely a hard limestone which takes a polish. Unlike other Purbeck beds it is crammed with the shells of small freshwater snails, and is sometimes crossed by white wandering 'lists' (cracks filled with calcite), or contains a scattering of white bivalves.

Near the foot of the limestone slope, punctuating the marble seam and born in part from the wealth it created, is a series of handsome manor farms. Only a short section survives of the bridleway once connecting them. It leaves the Valley Road to pass near Wilkeswood Farm, once the site of a small religious house and where Roman worked marble has been found. It continues in front of Quarr farmhouse, whose eastern wing is the remains of the 17th century manor house. The name fits since Quarr was heavily quarried for marble. Celia Fiennes would have seen its handsome cliffstone fireplace (dated 1651) for she was riding '...to Quare .... a relations house Cos'n Colliers'.

Here the bridleway quits the grit ridge to cross an often-boggy meadow where marble was dug in 1993 and 2004. Hard-going for carts, this must be a recent diversion. The old way followed the ridge-top footpath past a planner's dream – the ever neon-lit, terraced tarmac suburbia of Haycrafts Caravan Site – and passes Dunshay and Afflington Manor farms on the way to Corfe.

Dunshay was the manor house for Worth. The site is ancient, the present house dating from 1642 (marked on a drainpipe) when John Dolling rebuilt it. He probably planted the yew trees but the fine gateposts are early 18th century. Here lived Benjamin Jesty, the famous inoculator.

Dunshay was on Alice di Briwere's huge estates and she gifted its marble towards the building of Salisbury Cathedral between 1219 and 1231. North of the garden wall a deep water-logged pit is only part of the diggings. Mounds of overburden rise beyond it to continue beside a drive overshadowed by a rookery, once 'in towering elms', now in modest ash trees.

The present owner, the sculptor Mary Spencer Watson, has lived here since 1923. Her father, George Spencer Watson RA, a prominent portrait painter, lived partly in Studland from 1914. Her mother, Hilda, had her own mime theatre in London, and continued that work at Swanage's Mowlem Institute and at Dunshay. Their move to the house was delayed by a sitting tenant, the painter Lucy Kemp-Welch, famous for her pictures of horses. Mary remembers sprucing up her pony before a visit from the great lady.

'Elisha' and 'Elijah', 1938,
by Mary Spencer-Watson;
a section of Purbeck Marble

Dunshay became the heart of a flourishing set of creative folk. Henry Ford, illustrator of a famous 1920s series of fairy tales, settled in Dunshay Cottages. Visitors included Carl Jung, who had been persuaded to hold a summer school in a marquee on Ballard Estate. Hilda, having met him in Switzerland, invited him to tea. Mary recalls that he held forth on the myth Demeter and Persephone, then, turning to her, asked 'What do you make of it all?' Later, to his amusement, her donkey scraped her off by walking under a chain.

She started carving stone at thirteen, studied at The Royal Academy Schools then under Zadkine in Paris. Working mostly in Purbeck freestone, her latest works include the *Four Evangelists* commissioned for Wells Cathedral and Langton's *Purbeck Quarryman*. A retrospective exhibition took place at Salisbury in 2004.

During the war Mary worked the land. In September 1940 she was mowing a nearby field, using two retired circus horses, when German planes approached. One could hear the throb of engines some way off, and, in those early days, they came in daylight in skeins like geese. She took the ancient, unwieldy mower to the edge of the field and held the horses in case they should bolt. Being circus horses, they took it all in their stride. Then British fighters came, their trails visible in the cool air, shooting down bombers like lumbering turkeys.

In the 1930s Prince and Princess Troubetskoi settled in Haycrafts Lane, having escaped revolutionary Russia with little of their huge wealth. He spent his Purbeck life ragged and unsociable, tending the garden. She retained her royal bearing. By another marriage she had a concert pianist son who gave several recitals in Purbeck. When she died in 1958 Corfe Church hosted a Russian Orthodox funeral. A bearded priest and two women cantors came down from London. The weeping cortege, with its incense and candles, caused a stir as it passed along West Street to the cemetery.

Beyond Dunshay, Afflington stands beside the bridleway which goes south to Chapmans Pool. Most of the original house has gone, but its steeply-pointed gable is a 19th century version of a 17th century form. There was a village here, born no doubt of the mediaeval marble industry, which had a weekly market, an annual fair and, until 1547, a chapel. Uneven ground east of the house is all that remains. The Barnes family were long tenant farmers. Part of Kingston Estate, it was sold in 2004 in the aftermath of the Encombe sale, although Michael Barnes still farms much of the land. My great-grandmother rented the upper floor in 1935, and my mother's first foray into Purbeck was to join her grandmother for the summer holidays, while her parents were in India.

The 17th century manor-farm of Scoles, which has remnants of an early 14th century hall, stands further up the flank of the valley towards Kingston. It took its name from an earlier owner, William de Scovile. Away from any path, it is visited by design, not accident. Across Kingston Hill lies Blashenwell Farm (Blechenhamwelle in Saxon times) which was built in the late 18th century. The painter, Turner, climbed this hillside to sketch Corfe, the farm featuring in his foreground. Here a large spring used to turn a Victorian iron millwheel, which is still set in the wall beside the bridleway. Further down it created deep tufa deposits, centuries of gathered lime which have yielded mammal bones and mesolithic stone tools including an axe.

These manor houses mark older sites. Their owners benefited from the diggings that despoiled their fields as well as from crops, cattle and sheep. Mediaeval quarrymen attacked the land with confidence, in sure conviction of the glory of their God. It can never happen again. The shadow of a new figure, the planner, steps in to cripple industry with dreams of a frozen weekend playground. At the height of the marble industry old folk must have grieved for the green of spring scoured by great sores, piles of blue clay oozing down to discolour the meadows, to cloud their streams. The Black Country of its time, heavily-populated with strangers drawn to the quarries and masons' yards, is all green woodland now. The 13th and early 14th centuries saw its zenith. The air was loud with stone-work, and the roads towards Corfe busy with pedestrians, horses and stone-laden bullock carts.

Without marble Purbeck would have remained a backwater, notable only as a royal hunting ground. On the continent builders and masons were already using black Tournai stone for effigies, for contrast with the lightness of their building stones. Perhaps English masons sought some native material for a similar effect. The Romans had used the marble for mortars and inscribed slabs. When the Saxons and Normans dug Burr, a broken-shell limestone some three metres below the marble, they were daily reminded of those dark beds above. From the mid-12th century Purbeck Marble took the country by storm and was used for fonts, ledgers, coffin-lids and effigies. Slender polished shafts, featuring first in the late 12th century choir of Canterbury Cathedral, brought elegance and lightness to the massive stone piers that sustained the age of cathedrals. The piers of London's Temple Church, started around 1170, are the earliest surviving example of Purbeck marble taking a major structural role. The latest, too, since Trev's father quarried marble at Lynch to recreate it after the Blitz.

Using contemporary tools, each large fine-polished ledger took much time and labour. Some bore a decorative raised cross, its standard form indicating a common workshop in Purbeck. Some held brass figures and inscriptions manufactured in London, if not inset there. They were overshadowed by the skilled labour demanded for intricate mouldings and detailed tomb effigies required for princes and clergy. King John's effigy on his tomb at Worcester (c1240) came early, in the long reign of his son, Henry III. This voracious builder commissioned Edward the Confessor's shrine in Westminster Abbey, the climax of fine Purbeck marble work.

The beds outcropped near the surface but this block was soon dug. Masses of overburden had to be shifted, and the smooth line of the hillside was transformed as labourers followed the steep beds northwards into the earth. They were confronted by the water-table which, along with fashion, was the controlling factor. Few marble beds are more than 40cm thick. The recent digging at Quarr hit mediaeval workings, and some of their worked stone remained *in situ*, showing 'pit' marks just like those used until pneumatic drills came in. One large block, split but abandoned, had a steep-sided 'V', 15cm deep and more than 1.5m long punched into it, forming the line of weakness along which it was split. Perhaps it was for two coffins' lids or ledgers. Pillars were built up of sections cut on bed to be set up one above the other. Long, slender shafts were worked parallel to the bed.

Marble work succumbed to the Dissolution, Reformation and Puritan action during the Civil War. What remains indicates the size and importance of Purbeck's industrial past. In southeast England most mediaeval churches yield some marble. Few cathedrals do not.

It used to be assumed that all the marble block was shifted to Corfe for working but there is increasing evidence that much masonry work was carried near the quarry. Remnants of shafts, pillars, pillar bases, ledgers, pieces of sandstone for smoothing surfaces, as well as piles of 'scars' (fragments) have been found around Dunshay. In 1993 and 1994, when Judy Robson organised the rebuilding of a wall there, several worked pieces emerged from its fabric.

Much of the finest carving probably took place in Corfe workshops. Construction work has revealed deep banks of 'scars' in West Street and fragments of carvings are integrated into cottage walls. That the marble goods were shipped through Ower is commemorated each Shrove Tuesday when the Ancient Order of Marblers and Stonecutters take a pound of pepper to Ower Farm in payment for access to its long-vanished quay.

Purbeck Marble, iron-rich and vulnerable to oxidation, weathers badly in damp conditions. This must have played a part in its decline. It was displaced for fine effigies by Nottingham alabaster. Decline caused unemployment and led to a number of skilled men, called 'de Corfe', settling in London and elsewhere.

Since the mid-19th century the principal, albeit slight, demand for marble has been for restoration work. The bed is plentiful, and with modern machinery and pumps it is easy to replenish supplies. It must be dug early to dry it out before autumn. A fresh block, which is wet, is vulnerable to frost. A few local carvers, including Mike Bizley and Ian Ching work in marble.

★

Railway cuttings cross and recross the Valley Road. The railway's arrival in Swanage was no less revolutionary for being late. Carrying travellers, shifting stone and bringing in supplies, it became an essential part of life and the normal route to London. School pupils and commuters still used it in the 1960s. My first job, through the dramatic cold-spell of early 1963, entailed walking through the snow to the station. I used the journey to write letters before steaming into Poole. 'The scenery is white on either side of the lines as we rattle over the frozen rivers... We've just left Wareham behind - this is a through train.'

I remember the last passenger train hooting its way out of Swanage and the lines being taken up. It became a popular, attractive footpath, the one reversal of man's intrusion across Purbeck. Now there is no valley footpath into Swanage, save the one which lethally follows the road between Afflington, Corfe Common and from Crack Lane to Swanage. As the rails advanced through 1983 I was not alone in regretting the return of the train. But I use it, occasionally steaming into Corfe.

CORFE: TOWN AND CASTLE

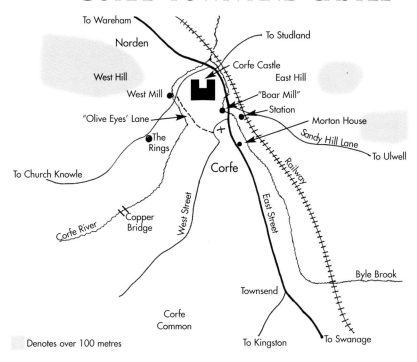

If, today, Swanage is Purbeck's main town, it has only recently risen out of the shadow of Corfe, with its royal castle and its two Members of Parliament granted by the first Elizabeth. Corfe Castle, guarding its double gap, is an image that typifies Purbeck. It is twice doubled, since 'Corfe' itself signifies 'gap'. Each passing tribe must have built on that hillock, so obvious for a defensive settlement. The hills on either side bear traces of occupation dating back to the Mesolithic. Some Roman remains have been discovered on the castle mound but, save for Saxon footings on the site of the great hall in the western Bailey, what stands today is entirely post-Conquest. The Normans began the castle around 1080, under William the Conqueror himself. He built masonry walls to the Inner Ward when much of the hilltop was only protected by a pallisade. Then, as fortresses are wont to, the castle descended its hill stage by stage. Around 1105, the Keep rose within the Inner Ward, and a further line of defences enclosed the inner Bailey. By 1200 the walls had advanced westwards, defending the spur on which the Great Hall rose from Saxon roots. A royal house was built within the Inner Ward. Henry III and Edward I continued the expansion. Finally, by the close of the 13th century, a great ditch plunged before the inner gate and walls, punctuated by bastions, replaced the palisade enclosing the Outer Bailey, a tongue of land to the southeast. Here stood the outer gateway and the bridge crossing the moat. The walls were of easily-accessible burr, the stone preferred by Saxons and Normans. The result was a grim stronghold – a dungeon casting heavy shadow on the folk below.

The castle was a place of horror for state victims; the assassination of King Edward in 978 being amongst the least of its atrocities. He has been depicted as an angelic youth but political expediency required his sanctity, and, so, saint he became. His body was shifted to Shaftesbury Abbey, and disappeared at the Dissolution. In 1931 excavations at Shaftesbury uncovered a lead casket, hastily concealed, containing the skeleton of a young man with injuries consistent with those described in accounts of the assassination. It was offered to the town but the councillors were doubtful so he now lies estranged in an Orthodox Church in Brookwood, dedicated in 1984 for his reception. The clergy, short of a saint or two, were not so choosey. Let's hope they got the right man. In 1978 Corfe was mobilised to commemorate the millennium of his assassination.

John's reign was particularly unsavoury for Corfe. After a rebellion in 1202 he held 24 French knights in Corfe's dungeons. Only two failed to starve to death. He had Peter the Hermit, a self-styled prophet, dragged to Wareham and back before hanging him off the walls. King Edward II was imprisoned here prior to his hideous end at Berkeley Castle. Many men passed in alive, out dead. Corfe Castle stands to represent all the fear and inhuman degradation man still inflicts on man. Children of Corfe grew up in that environment. It was not picturesque. Today that face is deeply buried beneath the romantic and colourful picture of Brave Dame Mary holding out against the humourless Puritans. She represented an era of such misrule that even the politically phlegmatic English were moved to rebel. Supporting despotism against democracy, she dressed brightly, held out bravely and there wasn't much blood spilled, anyhow.

Elizabeth sold Corfe, a state stronghold, to Sir Christopher Hatton (he of Hatton Gardens) who passed it to his nephew. His widow, after a couple more husbands, sold it, in 1635, to Sir John Bankes, who was rising steadily through the legal profession to become Lord Chief Justice of Common Pleas by 1640. Law brings riches, and that Sir John displayed his wealth, when furnishing the castle, is seen from his inventory of claimed losses drawn up at the Restoration. He risked his career (hoping to better it) by following Charles I to Oxford. His wife, Lady Mary Bankes, moved into the castle in 1642. The

A train runs along the valley from Swanage to Corfe

Left: Barry Audley shifting a large block of Purbeck Marble; Quarr Farm 2004

Digging exposes a neatly cut block left by mediaeval quarrymen; Quarr

The loss of a lovely footpath or the gain of a revived railway? Approaching Harmans Cross, 1982

Corfe Castle, a well-worn Purbeck icon; in winter

A Victorian cross dominates Corfe's market square, behind it the handsome post office

A piece of mediaeval worked marble in the wall above a doorway in West Street

The edge of Tyneham Great Wood towards Mupe Bay

Ancient sunken track from Creech descends into the valley with Gold Down as background

Over two metres high, the Harp Stone lurks in a hedge

Barrows crowning Nine Barrow Down

Windblown tree on the Ridge

Ballard Cliff, east end of the chalk ridge, overlooking Punfield Cove

Abandoned lime kiln at the foot of Knowle Hill

Littlesea; Richard Verge on our raft there in 1958

*The interior of St Nicholas's Church,
Studland*

*Treleven Haysom's Cross was set up on
an ancient sandstone base, Studland*

Conifers on Wytch Heath

The sluice bridge on Corfe River. There are initials and dates on the shields

Across Godlingston Heath to tilted Agglestone and Studland Bay

Looking south over Poole Harbour from Brownsea Island in 1963

A major fire affected much of the south of Brownsea in May 1963

Brands Bay from Redhorn Point at low tide

Holme Bridge crosses the Frome from Purbeck

*An old granary stands on the
customary nine staddle stones
(one removed) at West Creech Farm*

*From Creech Arch, the Folly,
looking through Great Wood
to Creech Grange*

Parliamentarians came the following spring, making several attempts to overcome the castle before besieging it. They used the church as a forward position, taking its lead for ammunition, and constructed two engines, The Sow and The Boar, to shelter them as they attacked the walls from the west. The Sow made several forays but was not proof against shot. Nine of the eleven men within her were hurt. One died. That discouraged the Boar. In August 1643 they gave up the attempt and left Corfe. Sir John died the following year but his widow held on. The siege resumed in early 1646 and, after 48 days, the castle fell through treachery. On 7th April 1646 Lt Col Pitman of the garrison persuaded the Governor to let in 50 men who were Parliamentary soldiers in disguise. Lady Bankes had little option but to surrender. She died soon after the Restoration. Her son, Sir Ralph, having regained the estate, vainly tried to recover the castle's furnishing and tapestries which had been carried off by Parliamentary officers who had been directed, by act of Parliament in 1647, to slight the walls. He solved his accommodation problem by building Kingston Lacy, where the gateless keys to the castle now lie. Weather has taken its toll of the building and the gale of 1866 sent much of Butavant Tower, weakened by gunpowder, rolling down the hill.

Even before it was destroyed the cliff-walled stronghold provided home for more than man. Denis Bond, in his *Chronicle,* writes for 1635: 'A Raven bred som tym before Christ dyd this yeare in Corfe Castell.' They always lay their eggs before Good Friday, and did so again, in 2004, when they raised young in an upper window of the castle ruins.

A 19th century map marks The Rings as 'Cromwell's Battery', perhaps a piece of historical memory now lost. As an earthwork on a slight eminence south of the Church Knowle road it was always a puzzle, comprising a little keep and bailey. It is generally overlooked, but, were it not for the castle, it would be an important local feature. It is thought to be the work of King Stephen's forces, a shelter from which to pursue an unsuccessful siege of the castle in 1139. Well situated for an assaulting force, perhaps it was also sty to those doomed siege machines, the Sow and the Boar.

The late 18th century search for the picturesque brought a changed assessment of dereliction. Perhaps survivors of the Grand Tour chose to glance at their own country's ruins. Corfe was sufficiently romantic to draw travellers. Turner came here in 1811 to draw the castle for his *Picturesque Views of Southern England.* His sketchbooks show that he looked at the castle from several directions. William Daniell, already famous for the collection of views he and his uncle painted in India between 1786 and 1794, came in 1823 to sketch for his *A Voyage Around Great Britain.* They were followed by many and variable painters. Perhaps they stayed several days, putting up at The Greyhound, as did other tourists of the time or, later, The Ship, which was rebuilt as The Bankes Arms. Both overlook the old market-place and are

A souvenir keyring;
two ravens

remarkable for a the single room supported by stone pillars which projects over both entrance and pavement. Heavy baggage could be passed up straight from a vehicle into this room, avoiding the narrow stairway.

Gerald White, looking out from the castle in 1855, mentions that 'those bare patches of red, white and yellow are clay diggings.' Then the clay industry was, along with agriculture, a major employer in Corfe. A clay digger told him that he earned 2 shillings a day - nothing when it rained. 'All are poor in Corfe', he said. White would have climbed unhindered to the castle from any direction he chose. In 1884 Corfe's poet, John Webber, in his *The Owl's Soliloquy*, gently mourns the fencing in of the castle. Soon they were charging. but there was no end to the picturesque. The turn of the 19th century saw artistic interest in Purbeck centred on Corfe, as well as Studland. Led by Wilson Steer, in 1908 members of the St Ives group came to the village to paint. Some artists stayed. Francis ('Fra') and Jessie Newbery settled at 112 East Street in 1918. He had been director of Glasgow School of Art and a friend of Charles Rennie Mackintosh who, with his wife, Margaret (connected, like Jessie, with Glasgow School of Embroidery), came to visit. 'Fra', having seen many of his best pupils slaughtered in the trenches, retired here sick with depression. His wife continued to work in textiles, and cut a notable figure in Corfe in her self-made dresses. Ada Cooper recalls them: '…a large man who wore a wide-brimmed hat, and she was a small woman who wore fantastic draperies in bright hues, quite strange to us in our more sober colours.' He painted several pictures using local people as his models, as in the altar-piece at Swanage Catholic Church. In Corfe he was notable for his portrayal of Edward the Martyr: in paint, on the village sign (1927), and, in stone, above the east gable of the church roof (1931). The church booklet states that he sculpted the roof figure. He did not. Walter Haysom carved it to his design, and he recalled the couple coming to inspect each stage. 'Fra' would suggest the next move, and his wife would totally disagree, leaving him in a quandary. Perhaps it would be fair to describe the result as tripartite.

Frances Hodgkins was prominent amongst 20th century painters settling in Corfe. She took an old chapel behind Haveland House, and spent the second world war there. Her paintings of this period often concerned modest buildings and courtyards but rarely the castle. Not noted for domestic skills, she shifted to The Greyhound where other folk could do her cooking and washing up. The attraction of Corfe has been tempered by the prohibitive cost of simple cottages. Nevertheless, two sculptors, Angelika Seik and Jonathan Sells, are based there.

There was music, too. The composer Kaikhosru Shapurji Sorabji, with his heavy glasses and gaberdeen mackintosh, was a figure of my youth. He settled at Townsend after composing his immense *Opus Clavicembalisticum,* in 1930. Then, although he continued to compose piano concertos, quintets and symphonies, he banned performance of his work until 1976. He had a sharp ear, often supporting *avant garde* composers long before they became fashionable.

At the turn of the century the Arts and Crafts movement, emphasising handicraft, swept Britain. Based at its epicentre, the Glasgow School of Art, the Newberys were sharply aware of Corfe's antecedents. The workshops for much of the finest marble carving were probably based around Corfe's West Street, and an early 14th century document refers to Purbeck marble as 'marbre de Corfe'. Writers comment on the great depths of marble 'scars' unearthed, along with broken work when trenches or foundations were dug. Corfe's historian-doctor, Dru Drury, talks of layers of marble debris (earlier writers say three or four metres deep) and a piece of shaft found when the water main was laid in 1924. A mediaeval carved piece of marble is set in the fabric above a door in West Street. Given the danger of loss or breakage inherent in transit, perhaps the very finest work was finished on site. Cottage industries worked marble, too, turning out mortars from Roman to mediaeval times. Roy Ford discovered marble debris, broken mortars and sandstone abrasives drawn from the Common when working on an outhouse in West Street.

As centre of carving astride the main route from quarry to port, Corfe's special relationship with the industry is acknowledged every Shrove Tuesday. On that day the Ancient Order of Marblers and Stone-Cutters holds its annual meeting. It claims an origin earlier than the Charter of 1651 it now holds. Many of its papers have been destroyed but its formal foundation could relate to the 17th century rise of a stone paving and tile industry. The meeting, an opportunity to unite on policy, seems to be more a social event. After a session at the Town Hall in which subjects are raised and discussed the members drink at The Fox, and kick a football along West Street. Amongst the formalities is the gift of pepper at Ower.

West Street, leading directly to the castle gate, was the main thoroughfare with the town hall, older cottages and shops. Many of its cottages have stonework taken from the castle ruins after its demolition. One, dated 1656, standing south of the east end of the path running beneath Castle Mound, is particularly rich in castle ashlar. It includes one Tudor fragment carved with a portcullis. That path beneath the castle rejoices in the name of Olive Eyes Lane but its origin is simple - it derives from Oliver Vye, 'Ollie Vye', an 18th century quarryman's name, not some lovely damsel.

Corfe Castle's ruins tower over the main road and rail route into the valley. Gone is the gaunt, forbidding aspect of its zenith. It has become a gentle money-spinning monument where trippers eat ice-creams, or pose for photographs in front of an icon of picturesque England. The tourists see fresh what I see jaded. It appealed to Enid Blyton, however. Didn't she choose the castle as a model in her *Five On a Treasure Island*? There is even a new Blyton shop to cash in on her passing. Due to its prohibitive charges local folk rarely visit the castle. When I went last, in 1983, for the sake of Indian friends, my father commented that he had not been since 1947. As kids, when it was thruppence under the benevolent Bankes regime, we climbed through the fence. Principle was involved, and that thruppence was better spent on éclairs. We would cycle there to wade along the river, netting small fish. Few of my friends lived in Corfe but, coming back from holidays and journeys, it remains the landmark: nearly home.

The modern town is distinguished for Dragon Bakery; The Fox, a favourite pub; a constant surge of tourists with video cameras, and exaggerated Christmas lights. Mortons House, now a hotel, was actually built by the Daccombe family in the late 16th century, and remains Corfe's finest domestic building. There is the handsome 18th century post office with a central bay running down through both stories, and a Town Hall which claimed to be the smallest in Britain. Corfe lost its two MPs with the Great

Reform Bill of 1832, and its status as borough the following year.

When the railway closed, Corfe station sank to utter dereliction although the yard continued to house a coal business. Its locks and shutters failed to keep people at bay. They broke in for shelter for the night, for romantic assignations, or a place for a quiet drink. In 1980 when Alex Miller and his partners decided to use it for their company they found it full of rubbish, the walls black with mould, the wooden floor of the waiting room burnt through by someone's fire. Taking it at a peppercorn rent they set to work to restore it, adding the authentic touch of British Railways paint. The business ran for ten years before succumbing to the recession but not before BBCTV found the station sufficiently authentic for the set of a John Buchan tale.

That wasn't the only time Corfe attracted film crews. Once, passing through on my motorbike, I glanced casually into the Square, as one does. It was alien, transformed by new facades, straw on the road and odd archaic people. Amazed, I narrowly missed a car going in the opposite direction. They were filming *The Mayor of Casterbridge*.

Beside the station is a little manufacturing quarter, the Sandy Hill Lane Industrial Centre. There, at least, life is in the present. Nick Crutchfield creates his eccentric, yet remarkably comfortable driftwood furniture; Tony Viney turns ever larger, ever thinner plates and bowls of Purbeck and Portland stones, and Kevin Vicars designs his signs.

Three water mills are marked on Corfe river in Tresswell's map of 1586. The united river powered Arfleet Mill, mediaeval 'Alfledesmulle', probably the most ancient. White mentions the combined Corfe river 'turning the wheel of Arcliffe (sic) Mill' but it disappeared under clay workings before WWI. Not far from it a well was recognised as holy in Roman times, two altars being set up there. Metal detectors found a field north of The National Trust centre to be scattered with Roman coins. There was also reputed to be a holy spring near Norden where Edward fell.

The eastern tributary passes through the last survivor, now called Boar Mill, perhaps reviving an old name, yet driven by a turbine in its final days. Its elongated triangular pond is now overgrown. It stands beside the main road as it descends from the Square. The last owner was determined to keep it from The National Trust, but the legal profession soon managed to circumvent the conditions of the old lady's will. Moral standards were never a part of heritage.

West Mill, now almost gone, stood near Olive Eyes Lane's opening onto the bridge. Active until 1790, it became a pair of cottages which were demolished around 1920; it was worked by the main, west tributary. Whether officially 'Wicken', 'Steeple Brook' or 'the Lake', it remained Corfe river to us as it had to Hutchins. It rises beyond Steeple and its basin carved most of the western part of Purbeck's valley.

THE VALLEY WEST OF CORFE

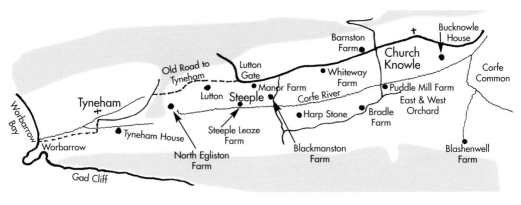

Denotes over 100 metres

The main body of the Corfe River rises within the army firing range, near North Egliston Farm, as does another brook flowing in the opposite direction through Tyneham to Worbarrow Bay. Together their systems formed the western valley, which is partially divided from the eastern by Corfe Common, an extension of the Valley Road ridge. Uncultivated, the Common's sandy heart creates and sustains an isolated upland of semi-heath complete with heather south of Corfe. It is crossed by the Kingston road and bordered to the south and west by the brook from Dunshay, which turns abruptly to join the west tributary of the Corfe River.

Bronze Age folk buried their dead in round barrows on the crest of the Common. Never divided up between landowners, it still serves as rough grazing, crossed by sunken tracks, fading and reappearing as they head for the south end of West Street. Pits sunk in the summit yielded sandstone for honing tools as well as abrasives to remove tool-marks from worked marble.

Finer grades of abrasive to create a polish were probably imported and must be preserved amongst workshop detritus. The marble narrows westwards, as does the valley, and handsome manor houses no longer punctuate it.

A footpath leads past Corfe's new cemetery towards Bucknowle, crossing the stream by a neat little 17th century Copper Bridge. In a field beyond, an amateur archaeologist, Tony Brown, noticed Roman pottery. Excavations between 1976 and 1991 revealed the plan of a Roman villa, the first found south of the chalk ridge. They found 2nd- to late 4th century coins, a tessellated pavement and evidence that the site was inhabited well before Roman times. Purbeck's villas were probably those of Romanised Celts, not Italian colonists.

Beyond, Bucknowle House, set back on a low hill south of the road, typified a Victorian turn to the architectural past with its large Tudor chimneys. The road winds on into Church Knowle, the largest settlement in this part of the valley. Its name derived from the church of St Peter, dating from the 13th century onwards, which stands on a little artificial knowle.

North of the chancel arch is a monument to John Clavell (1541-1609) and his two wives, which he erected 37 years before his death. This reflected practicality rather than morbidity. His first wife, dying in 1571, required a tomb befitting her status and he prepared for an inevitable future beside her. The canopied tomb is made of Portland stone, following a form popular at the close of the Purbeck Marble era. It is almost identical to the marble Skerne tomb in Bere Regis church. Three brasses show John Clavell (centre), his first wife with her children (left), and second wife (right), her arms bearing three nice leopard faces. Then childless, she went on to produce eight children. Three wall memorials commemorate Mansels who died abroad: one in Australia, and two who died in successive years during the First World War - one at sea, the other in the carnage of France.

The church mound slopes steeply on the south and east. Northwards, it melds into meadow. The road in front loops to accommodate the garden of another handsome Victorian rectory, rebuilt in 1852, again with an eye towards the Tudor period. It stresses the enormous distance 19th century Anglicanism strayed from Christ's teaching. No rural Victorian church seemed complete without a pile nearby for the gentleman vicar, his family and staff.

The local pub, the New Inn was adapted from an 18th century house, some saying that the public bar was once a dairy. A popular venue with the younger generation in the sixties, it suffered from a diminishing local clientele as the village community faded. Ever stricter drink-driving laws make life harder for such businesses but, as the sole pub in this area with the added attraction of providing meals, it serves as a place to stop on a walk or drive.

The Animal Sanctuary, founded with a legacy from Margaret Green, has become an important landmark in Church Knowle, and a destination for many injured or unwanted beasts. I walked over there several years ago, carrying in my jacket an immature Razorbill, found oiled. Once cleaned it became remarkably tame but I had to pass it on before starting a new job. A gentle, peaceful bird until then, it spent much of that walk justifying its name.

At the foot of the pass over the ridge at Cocknowle is Barnston Manor, long the seat of the Clavells but sold in an attempt to clear Sir William's debts. It rivals Godlingston in age, being built in the 13th century by the d'Estoke family. The name derives from a Saxon thane, Berne, who held the land. Most of the ground floor dates from the 13th century. The western section was thought to be a later addition but restoration work revealed a typical 13th century stone window-surround *in situ* beneath plaster. Spiral stairs lead to an upper floor and a fine Tudor room with an oriel window. It used to be a farmhouse and remained as such into the 1960s. For several years during the 1970s it was leased by Peter and Lyn Avery, who made it a venue for plays, exhibitions and music. I remember several summer evenings admiring the house and its garden during breaks in the productions, but have forgotten the performances.

The valley here shows traces of extinct settlements belonging to a busy Iron Age agricultural population. Some thrived into the middle-ages and most are marked by later farmhouses. Apart from Barnston and Bucknowle there were hamlets at West and East Bradle, West and East Orchard and at Hurpston. Further west, Whiteway has seen better days, a village surviving west of the farm until around 1600. Terry Lucas, indicating the 17th century sealed doorways at his home, Quarr Farm, commented that those of surviving cottages at Whiteway are identical. There were mills along the stream, too, at Puddlemill and Hurpston, but little evidence marks their passing.

Two roads rise out of the valley to unite on the limestone ridge and descend into Kimmeridge. From their confluence a sunken track runs north through woodland. In the hedgerow on its western side, placed there by who knows whom or when, stands a great slab of burr known as the Harpstone. The area was know as Herpston in 1340. Neither settlement nor stone features in the Domesday Book. Perhaps it was merely as a marker between two estates but its very size has ordained it with magical properties. Roughly rectangular and not obviously shaped, it stands over 2m high and 1m wide. New Age worshippers come here, leaving feathers and coins in the niches, so characteristic of burr, and nightlights or candles whose wax gutters down its surface. Peter Knight, in his *Ancient Stones of Dorset*, mentions a strange warmth halfway up it, which quite eludes me. It marks no obvious pious site and, well down into the valley, it is not the prominent landmark it might have been.

That sunken track fades as it crosses the valley floor, but re-emerges almost opposite as a bridleway rising the north slope to cross the ridge towards Creech Barrow. It avoids Blackmanston farm, old in itself, which stands by the west road to Kimmeridge near where it crosses a little bridge over the stream. 'TC 1824' is deeply inscribed in its parapet. An Elizabethan Manor house, Blackmanston almost turns its back on the road to face an older route, the footpath to Steeple. Bought by the Clavells, it remains part of Smedmore Estate.

A path leads from Blackmanston straight to Steeple Church. A tiny hamlet, Steeple has its own manor house, bearing the date 1698 and the crest of the Clavells, who bought it in 1567 from the Lawrences. Perched on a hillock, visible from afar and out of all proportion to its present settlement, the church reflects a faded population. It origins are ancient, the nave and south doorway being 12th century, but, like every old church, it has additions and alterations. Mural painting catches my eye, and there is a small patch of floral decoration at the top of the north wall. Decline must have been well-advanced in 1721, when the living was combined with Tyneham's.

A Purbeck marble ledger in the sanctuary is inscribed to Denis Bond Esq. of Grange, who died in 1746. Denis brought wealth and dishonour to the family. The ledger is probably secondhand, re-used from a long-forgotten, once distinguished, mediaeval burial. In the north transept, there stands a barrel organ, bought for the church in 1858 by Nathaniel Bond, rector for almost forty years. It cost 100 guineas including transport from Wareham and was still in working order in 1910. Later it was used to provide parts for the pipe, only to be restored in the 1990s. Even here, a memorial from the First World War lists six men, most of them under thirty.

After the Dissolution, Sir Oliver Lawrence acquired the manor. A 14th century marriage with the Washington clan makes Steeple church famous across the Atlantic. On a carved tablet dated 1616 and set above the east doorway to the north transept a coat of arms shows the Washington stars and stripes coupled with the ragged cross of the Lawrences. Americans stationed nearby prior to the Normandy landings sometimes turned up here to worship, in deference to the connection.

From the church a footpath leads to Steepleleaze Farm, joining the bridleway across the valley to become the road to Creech and East Lulworth. This is the frontier of red flag territory, subject to the vagaries of the Ministry of Defence. The right-angle in the valley road at Lutton Gate once marked the northern limb of a crossroads. Westwards lies the old way to Tyneham, passing Lutton and North Egliston Farms before joining the modern road. Closed since the year of my birth it is hard to visualise the valley as anything but forbidden, and, yet, horses, carts and cars once passed freely that way, providing one stopped to open several gates. How many of the original

A pair of binoculars; a Comma butterfly

inhabitants or their heirs would be living there now, if the evacuation of 1943 had never happened? Would there be a busy flow of traffic on fine Fridays to light up the weekend cottages? Local landowners temper the Purbeck clearances. The National Trust and the market have a stomach but no heart. The Bonds might well have favoured local tenants against the highest bidder.

★

As boys, Trev and I approached Tyneham from Brandy Bay up the path in that grassy, uneven angle between Gad Cliff and the unstable shale. Like the smugglers who preceded us we were briefly vulnerable when breaking the skyline at the clifftop and the hilltop above but the shelter of Tyneham Great Wood was close. Less burdened than smugglers we could disappear if there was anyone around.

Later, we sometimes took the old road, always alert, leaving it for the steep-sided gwyle running down to the sea. Sometimes we stopped to nose round the empty, still used farm buildings. Lutton was the first Purbeck home of the Bonds, who possibly settled there in 1431, but were certainly established by 1501. The present buildings don't predate the 17th century. According to a letter sent to Ralph Bankes after the Restoration, timbers from Corfe Castle's great hall were carried here and are said to support the barn roof. Once we noticed a sailing vessel cut into a timber but failed to find it again.

The worst punishment, in the late fifties, was to be taken to the guard-room at Lulworth to give our details. We never suffered it. We were caught once, however, but not until we were in our twenties. John had brought a girl with him and, when we were spotted, she couldn't run. We sheltered in a farm building. I stood in a corner by the door, while the others crouched opposite. A dog came into the farmyard, entered our building, sniffed and wandered out. A young officer shouted 'Come out, children. I know you're there!' He must have just glimpsed us. Finally, he came through the doorway and, seeing the others, asked them what they were up to. Since they didn't answer I did, from behind his shoulder. It was a bad tactical error on his part not to notice me. Perhaps that was why he just told us to leave.

Celia Fiennes would have ridden along the south ridge from Quarr: '...att Tinnum Lady Lawrences there is a pretty large house but very old timber built.' The Bonds were not yet established and the widowed mistress of the house, preferring her titled name, had remarried to become Mrs Culliford. At least both husbands were Robert.

Ralph Bond, the last squire, was not the eldest son, but his brother had died in India, leaving him to inherit Tyneham in 1935. The future seemed secure. Then came war. The valley was requisitioned in 1943, just as his son had been declared lost, later to be found, in Italy. Given 28 days to evacuate 'for the duration', the Tyneham folk moved in the security of patriotic duty and a government promise. Hitler was not alone in his ability to tear up scraps of paper.

Looting started soon after Tyneham's inhabitants were evicted. It sits sadly with the vision of 'Our Finest Hour'. Beneath the propaganda folk continued business as usual. Heavy household articles disappeared even before householders could arrange to collect them. The lead from Tyneham House was stolen soon after the war, accelerating decay. Who had that? The saga shows two faces of humanity: brave submission to the common good juxtaposed against selfish greed.

Ralph died in 1952, as his nephew, Martin Bond, recalled, 'bitterly unreconciled to the loss of Tyneham and deeply wounded by the Government's shabby behaviour and broken promise to return Tyneham to him and its former inhabitants.'

When we first intruded, Tyneham House still stood in decaying glory. It was spring, and a disturbed buzzard mewed as it circled above the fresh green leaves. That glorious mewing, a common sound now, was rare forty years back. The lawn, tended for centuries, still stubbornly retained some genteel quality, and the daffodils had not returned to their wild form. Tyneham seemed to me as though it had always been abandoned - abandonment being its natural state. We were kids, and the fifteen years the army had held it was a lifetime.

In my mind the still-standing house sits permanently in spring. It was not always spring, of course, but the first time is so clear, and it was the season we most often intruded on the untouched peace of the place. There I first saw a haha, an artificial fall from the garden in front of the house, which dispensed with a disfiguring fence to separate the garden's flowers from the cattle beyond.

In those early days the cottages were simply ruined. They kept their roofs, but usually they had fallen in, aided by weather and gunfire. There was broken glass in windows and falling wallpaper. The church was locked but one could wander from room to room in the Rectory until a mysterious fire destroyed it. For a glimpse of the living community, Lilian Bond's *Tyneham* is unrivalled. We saw it dead, musty and decaying, as yet not mummified. That came later when, as a prelude to opening the valley more regularly to the public, the ruins were levelled or 'made safe'.

In 1968 lorry-loads of stonework were carried away as Tyneham House was dismantled. It was left a ruin, its façade destroyed. The next spring a kestrel, nesting in an upstairs fireplace, flew out, abusing us. The prettiest masonry passed to a peer and a Tory MP. Were they generously housing it for us or greedily indulging themselves? Martin Bond seems in little doubt: 'Enterprising people in public positions "saved" pieces of Tyneham to enhance houses like Bingham's Melcombe & Athelhampton.' During the Civil War Bingham's Melcombe had 'saved' from Corfe Castle, too. Lost among the trees, little remains now but a wrecked shell, that cast-iron fireplace set pointlessly in mid-air. The track, one of Tyneham's arteries, that once led to it is overgrown. The woodland remains glorious in spring with great horse chestnuts bearing bright candles, beneath them snowdrops, then daffodils and primroses giving way to bluebells and wild garlic. Both Sika and Roe deer wander there.

Whilst demolishing the 16th century fabric of Tyneham House, rich in good stonework, they left the 14th century hall raised on a high plinth and projecting from its rear. Historically the most interesting part, it had the least interesting masonry - save for the doorway, which has gone. Its pitched roof was sustained by a timber structure of ogee and cusped arches, immediately relating to my work in India. A series of little arcs, pointed at its centre, and cusped arches were popular in the reign of Shah Jahan, builder of the Taj Mahal (1632-43). Not that the emperor came to Tyneham: both share a common Middle Eastern Islamic origin. That arch passed east across the Islamic world and west, with crusaders and pilgrims, to late Gothic architecture. The timberwork remains, as do the flagged floor and a stone staircase, now destined nowhere. Where are the valuable stone roof-tiles now, which were replaced with corrugated iron to lighten the load?

The author Monica Hutchings started a movement aimed at forcing the government to release Tyneham. I never supported it. The choice was clear: it could stay as it was, which required no movement, or be vacated and succumb to intensive agriculture and holiday cottages. Administered by some dead bureaucratic hand, it would no longer be the wonderful, exciting wilderness that military occupation has made it. Beasts, butterflies and birds flourished, more secure and content under gunfire than in the rest of Purbeck with its cars and sprays.

Mary remembers the living house. She and her mother rode over from Dunshay to visit the Bonds at Tyneham, a pony carrying their camping things. They took the bridleway following the ridge above Smedmore, Kimmeridge and South Egliston before descending towards the house. The beauties of rugged scenery were yet to strike Europe when Fiennes passed by. Nature was not yet picturesque, still hostile and very incompletely mastered. By Mary's day the sea, cliffs and the very wildness had become Purbeck's main attraction. More intensive agriculture had cut the valley route, setting up gates and a motor road, already dangerous for horses. She remembers the projecting porch, more vividly a large copy of a Rubens painting which dominated the dining room. This must have been Gainsborough's copy of *The Descent from the Cross*.

Later, Mary and her mother rose up onto the opposite ridge, the chalk hills past Flowers Barrow, with difficulty persuading the pony carrying their baggage to descend to Arish Mell. They were heading west to Chaldon to meet the sculptor, Elizabeth Muntz. That abrupt-sided ridge, its local stretch shown in maps as the Purbeck Hills, runs across much of south Dorset. From Flowers Barrow to Ballard it forms the central spine of Purbeck.

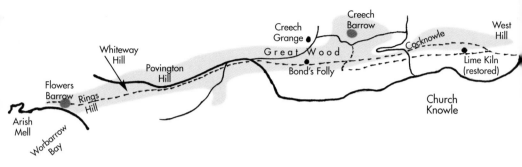

Denotes over 100 metres

THE RIDGE:
FLOWERS BARROW TO OLD HARRY

A wall of chalk, tilted to form a prominent ridge outcrops along the south coast of England. Often the sea has eaten away softer deposits to be held back by this resilient barrier. It is an illustration of strength in numbers, for chalk consists of incredible billions of coccoliths, single-celled calcareous plants that each, in dying, added its puff of dust to the mass. Rivers forming the Solent detached a strip of that ridge as the backbone of the Isle of Wight. At the Needles the white cliffs gaze out over sixteen miles of sea to a reflection, Ballard Point. From there the spine runs hog-backed across Purbeck to Flowers Barrow to be almost cut again at Arish Mell, the island's western extremity. Here only a tiny brook separates Purbeck from the rest of Dorset but it was the same sort of gap as the Solent, and that brook became sea. The army has been established longer on the chalk rise of Bindon Hill, west of Purbeck's border. War gave it the opportunity to advance eastwards in search of *lebensraum*.

The ascent onto Rings Hill rewards the effort. Not only is the view formidable but the ridge is crowned by an ancient fortress, Flowers Barrow, comprising two concentric earth ramparts once reinforced with timber. The name has changed little in 700 years but its origin remains vague. Why the Flowers? A bird's-eye view shows a smaller but yet impressive version of Maiden Castle, an elongated enclosure devoured to the south by retreating

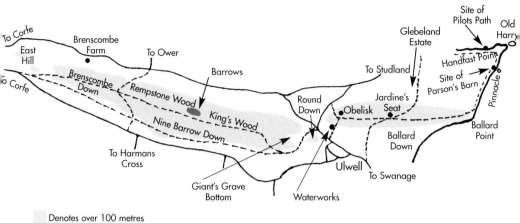

cliffs. The innermost rampart, which was built earlier, enclosed a settlement. Traces of its huts are marked by oval platforms. When it thrived, was it seen as a fortress or a normal walled settlement in unsettled times? In the southeast an opening through the outer wall leads towards, but, for defensive reasons, not directly into, another break through the inner wall.

Flowers Barrow came to me late. It stood too prominent on the skyline – a strategic site for those ancient folk being strategically vulnerable for us boys who had learnt to trespass gently. The men who occupied and defended it probably strengthened it further with a palisade of timbers drawn from the woods below, with spiked posts to further impede attack. From here they hoped to stay all rivals. Eventually, in 43 AD, Vespasian came and they failed. Amongst Iron Age remains found here were sling stones, too meek to hold the Romans. Rusty practice shells, a newer generation of missiles, lie to the north. Flowers Barrow stood as a wild and magnificent surprise to me when the army finally (and only occasionally) opened the coastal path.

To walk along the crest, through the gorse, is to follow a well-worn track, busy when the valley was overgrown and difficult to pass. Choosing a fine day, little Turner would have taken this route. Finished with views of Corfe Castle, he was bound for the next dramatic venue, Lulworth Cove. White, also bound for Lulworth, followed it in fog and optimistically descended from the ridge too early, only to wander happily into Tyneham. The ridgeway remains a convenient track for those unburdened with cars. It runs parallel for a while to the Lulworth road, crossing the road descending into Tyneham valley and that over the hill from Lutton Gate to Creech Grange. The first time we cycled down the north side of the ridge towards Lulworth Trev had a puncture. Unprepared, we stuffed the tyre full of grass. It didn't work. Luckily we met a boy from school who lent us ten shillings for the repair.

A handsome hanger wood, rich in ash and beech, runs along much of the north flank. The Creech road descends through it, past smooth beeches that are glorious green in spring and copper in autumn. Alone, that was my favourite way to approach the military heathland. The path may be tedious, but the woodland is beautiful: full of bluebells and wild garlic in spring, cool in the warmth of summer and stark and shapely in winter. A buzzard would rise from its nest to appear at intervals between the leaf canopy, wheeling and mewing, until I was well clear. Once a goshawk, a sly rarity hereabouts, slipped past me through the trees. There were always deer, shrieking or fleeing white-scutted in clattering panic. Quitting the wood at its western end I came out into rough meadow near the whiteness of the greatest active clay pit and deep within the range.

There is a sinister aspect to the crest of the ridge, talk of a Lost Legion marching at midnight. It is one of those phenomena people half believe and never witness, but know of others, unmet, who have. Did something happen that December night, in 1678, or was it all drunken fantasy? As Hutchins tells it, Captain John Lawrence, his brother and 100 other people, all living north of the ridge around Creech Grange saw, as well as heard, a party of several thousand armed men marching from Flowers Barrow over Grange Hill. The effect was such that village folk fled to Wareham. There boats were moved to the north bank of the Frome and the bridge was barricaded to prevent a crossing by invaders. It was the time of Titus Oates, our very own McCarthy, bringing fears of a Papist Plot. Three hundred militia were posted to Wareham and the Lawrence brothers galloped to London to describe on oath before the Council what had happened. Nothing more was seen. The troops with their clanking armour disappeared into thin air. Since then others, claiming to have witnessed similar if more modest phenomena, keep the Lost Legion alive. That army officers on the Ranges are among them adds plausibility to the yarn.

The hanger wood runs east of the road, too, cut beneath Bond's Folly to render it visible in silhouette from Creech Grange. An arid, pointless structure of pillars and arches, a pinch of the Picturesque, it was set up in 1740 by the Denis Bond who lies in Steeple Church. From its foot the house is hidden but there is a fine view from the top.

The ridge yields flint, which can only be created in chalk. Its conchoidal fracture forms sharp, long-lasting blades. It became an essential trade commodity to Stone Age man, and an added attraction of the chalk uplands. Early artisans, crouched overlooking a potentially hostile world, patiently chipped tools with a glorious skill. For functional beauty, look at a flint axe. To later man the chalk itself yielded high-quality lime, which was valuable

Grange Arch, the folly above Creech; a flint axe

for mettling roads or liming soil. Chalk pits, old and new, punctuate the ridge's flanks and there are remnants of lime kilns.

Chalk downland is an impoverished, highly alkaline environment, sparse of soil and porous. It is also liable to desiccation, and supports a unique flora in a matrix of short, tough turf, sustaining its own spectrum of creatures. A rich range of butterflies benefits from the poverty of the soil: it was never worth spraying. Although early folk lived and farmed here it is now thought fit only for grazing sheep. Mesolithic Man preferred it, and was both attracted by the vantage point and discouraged from the valley by its thick, deep-rooted undergowth. From the late Stone Age through the Bronze Age, men raised barrows here over their dead chiefs. Iron Age Celts divided it into fields with low earth walls, terraced the lower levels with lynchets. Both are still visible despite the ploughing grants prior to 1972 which served to flatten many profiles. It was Celtic Durotrigians who held the ridge when the Romans came.

A single anomalous hill rises separate yet prominent against the north flank, taller than the ridge. From Wareham, it appears almost volcanic; from the valley to the south it is a peak, peering over smooth downland. Its name, Creech Barrow, stresses the strange effect, both words meaning 'hill'. It is not of chalk but much younger iron-rich grit, and the plants it bears are akin to those of the heathland beyond. Those Bagshot beds interpolate such coarse sands with lenses of pure clay, which, prior to oil, was the great mineral resource of north Purbeck. Beneath the hill clay was mined until underground working ceased in the 1990s. Sand was dug from the other side of the hill: they say that man's tunnelling has caused its peak to sink six metres.

Creech Barrow was a viewpoint for the living as for the dead. Next to a Bronze Age barrow, on its peak, are clear footings of a later building, said to be one of King John's hunting lodges. There are strange earthworks too. Man has continually tampered with this topography, leaving furrows and embankments on the adjoining ridge, and more mysterious pillow mounds above Barnston.

East of Creech Barrow the road from Church Knowle to Furzebrook takes a spectacular hairpin through a steep-sided dry valley, where a great chalk pit blazed from the hill, supplying mettle for claypit tracks. There are traces of a cable railway here, constructed in the 1880s, using gravity to carry lime rich marl to the Wareham Cement Works at Ridge.

It was only when I had a moped, bought with £11 gained from selling the lead encasing old cable when our house was rewired, that the ridge west of Corfe became easily accessible and familiar. East of Corfe we had known the downs from childhood. Ballard and Nine Barrow were stalwart regulars for family walks. In summer my mother occasionally walked the four of us along the hill to Corfe, at lunchtime unveiling a cold chicken, a rare luxury in the early fifties. The day was perfected with the train journey back to Swanage and the tired mile home. One springtime at dusk I was taken to watch my first badgers at a sett in a chalk pit just above Knitson Farm. The beautiful wild creatures, oblivious of our presence, nosed past through the dry grass within touching distance.

East and West Hill, overlooking Corfe Castle from either side, must have been busy during every attack on the castle. King Stephen's forces, then those of Parliament, would have swarmed there, spying into the defences. When my father came back from WWII, he would discuss with my elder brother what manner of ordnance (and at which angle) would pick off that tower or those sheep. Meanwhile I chased butterflies. Below East Hill, beside the road to Studland, is a waterworks that feeds a resevoir buried in the hillside. Coloured dyes show that its catchment area stretches as far as the uplands near Blandford.

Traffic from Corfe to Ulwell and Studland often took the hilltop route as far as the Ulwell gap. Old routes up to and over the ridge survive as bridleways. Often, to avoid a dog leg, I choose that over Brenscombe Hill which runs down through the hanger wood towards Rempstone and Ower Quay. In spring the woods there are spread with bluebells, dog mercury and bright green spurge, and at night the darkness moves with conflicting smells. Another track rises from Knitson to reach the heath and harbour through Kingswood. The market at Poole was important to Purbeck folk, and these routes led to the ferry-boats that took them there.

Above Knitson the highest point on the ridge just fails to reach 200m. The biggest concentration of barrows in Purbeck stand some ten metres lower. These are Bronze Age round barrows which, set in a row, increase in size eastwards, then fade again. The first, scarcely discernible, leads to two great raised hemispheres. Next to them, and parallel to the row and the hill's axis, stands Purbeck's only Stone Age Long Barrow, built to cover several burials. To us this whole stretch of the hill is Nine Barrow Down (North Hill for Langton folk) although fourteen barrows are listed. Was this a sacred place with a shrine tended by a priest? Or was it merely a traditional burial site, abandoned between interments? Free of the burden of organised religion it has held a certain sanctity for me since first leaving Purbeck to travel. In the last days before a long trip I come here to sit, think and wish. Is it merely because the settings for so much of my life are visible below?

On Godlingston Down a couple of large WWII concrete bunkers re-main intact. One, just before the track descends to Ulwell, gives a wonderful view of Swanage and its bay. When it was used for storing hay I slept there several times, perhaps returning from a summer party. Now livestock stray in from bad weather, leaving the floor richer for their passing. The second, less hospitable, is below at the foot of the hill. Rude pylons, horrid monuments to the stranglehold of modern communication, rise above the descents to Corfe and Ulwell.

The ridge breaks before Ulwell, with the chalk road descending to cross a gap past Giant's Grave Bottom (long used as a particularly safe rifle range), to join the Swanage-Studland road. More prosaically, the bifurcation in the hill around the bottom is Forked Down. Isolated between this gap and that of Ulwell, hemispherical Round Down is a riverless reminiscence of Corfe's Castle Mound. Across the main road is another waterworks at the foot of Ballard Down which pumps water up to a reservoir. According to W.M.Hardy, Jenny Gould's Cottage, a smugglers' rendezvous, was some-where between here and Currendon Hill. Hundreds of tubs of liquor were stored there on their way to Poole. The house and land, held by the Church Land's Trust, faded away in the early 19th century, perhaps both somehow embezzled.

An earliest memory, when I was a little boy in bed, is waking to see the black night cut by marching red fire. They were swaying too wildly on

Ballard Down. When we were older, we were taken for walks along its summit, past brick buildings left from the war, beside concrete steps leading into the bowels of the earth. Never properly cleared, the remnants survive next to the sets of four bases of little pylons. Another piece of war wreckage was the granite obelisk set up by George Burt in 1892 to glorify his getting Swanage's water supply on line. It was another of his collection of bits of London monuments, the pair to that at Smedmore. He chose to perch it on a Bronze Age barrow. The chieftain shrugged at his presumption, and it collapsed, but he persisted. They knocked it down early in the war in case it should be a landmark, simultaneously erecting far taller pylons at Worth. In 1973, the army re-erected it.

So near home, Ballard, as 'up on the downs', was a regular playground. We went birds-nesting in the hedges along its foot; caught butterflies over the richly-scented wild marjoram above the waterworks, and reptiles, including smooth snakes, from beneath pieces of corrugated iron. Later we went shooting rabbits or pigeons. The hilltop was made for flying kites. At Ulwell Farm there was a cache of ancient deck-chair canvas. Using bamboo bean sticks we turned it into an immense kite and released it into a brisk breeze. The balance was bad, sending it straight for the ground. It needed a tail. Someone suggested our jerseys tied in a row. That worked. The kite rose ever higher until the wind, with an extra tug, broke the string. It sailed away, swaying, gliding far out over the fields before hitting the ground. We followed it, not daring to go home without our jerseys.

The track over the centre of Ballard Down, a convenient route between Swanage and Studland, was always busy. At its summit lies a badly-cracked oblong block of stone deeply incised with the words 'Rest and be Thankful'. Set up by one Dr Jardine in 1852 it is low-key, peacefully passed or happily sat upon. There were others. The Scotts had 'Eldon's Seat' at Encombe, but they had right of ownership; the Bonds' 'Ocean Seat' above Brandy Bay came later. A storm of stone seats has followed.

There were more barrows along Ballard, but ploughing and wartime structures reduced or levelled them. Further on, approaching the sea, the hill falls away sharply to the south creating a chalk face which is steeper than it looks. Grass and, in season, pink valerian grow up it, giving it an air of gentleness and enticing people to climb. It becomes progressively more difficult until, looking back, the horror of the situation is apparent. It is not far short of sheer. Amongst the many to be nearly stuck halfway, I know how that backward look feels.

I have seen Ballard's cliff, another symbol of home, loom out of the full moon night as the ferry glided in from Cherbourg. From the sea, in daytime, the startling Isle of Purbeck Thrust Fault curves down the face of the cliff, moving the strata from vertical to horizontal, in one swoop. That ill-consolidated chalk is dangerous. Exploring, we scrambled as far as possible along the shore beneath to a cave complete with shingle beach sheltered by a long rock, a little short of Ballard Point. The hazard was a regular fall of boulders from above. One exploding on a rock beside my sister discouraged me. We used to go out along the cliffs beyond, looking for gulls' eggs or simply bird-watching. Once, leaning over to look at nests on a grassy ledge, Robert's satchel slipped, bounced twice and disappeared into infinity. That should have been a warning. When we were fourteen, Macky and I climbed down at the highest stretch of cliff. It was 11th September, and I was leading until the going became tricky. Then he, a better climber, took over. The large piece of rock which he was gripping gave way and he fell to his death. I stayed clear of those cliffs for decades, and still sometimes wake with the nightmare.

I have a childhood memory of a ship, lodged on the end of the headland and visible from Swanage, but it doesn't seem to tie with any real event. Did it happen? Childhood is so unclear and stories merge seamlessly with reality. They took me out to see gliders head for Normandy. I was only a year old but told so often, I feel the picture is retained.

There was a smaller wreck of my own there, which happened whilst rowing two friends in a dinghy. The sea was calm but for a deceptive swell. All three were smoking when a wave breaking on a submerged rock swamped us. Perhaps it was Argyle Rock, the one that sank the *Argyle* two centuries earlier. Spitting out our sodden fags we rowed with difficulty to the shore below the cliff, the oars of the sunken boat floating out of the rowlocks. Long before, Trev's father took a boat with some friends to shoot cormorants along Ballard cliffs. One careless man shot through the bottom boards. They staggered back to Swanage.

The cormorants, nesting here and feeding in Poole Harbour, were shot, as rivals, by fishermen who claimed a government bounty. Since that ceased numbers have risen. We counted 77 nests in 1983, and 122 in 1994. They taint the sea breeze along the clifftop with the stink of guano. The real sea-birds no longer nest here, but there are ravens, peregrines, shags, great black backed and herring gulls. There was even a little colony of house martins near Handfast Point in the early 1980s.

The great cave, Parsons Barn, at the lower, northern end of the cliffs, collapsed in 1963. Discussing the name, Trev mentioned that cormorants were called 'Isle of Wight Parsons' from the cloak-like appearance of their drying wings. Parsons Barn is claimed as the venue for a seizure of smuggled tea. That tale seems to be an embellishment of an event in 1747, when a major seizure at sea inspired smugglers to attack Poole Custom House where it was impounded. They regained a large amount of it, but later many were arrested and six hanged.

It is here, at Handfast Point, that the stacks rise. The pointed Pinnacle was, they say, home to the local peregrine, but it has always preferred dry land in my time. Two more were known as Old Harry and his wife, but the wife was reduced to a stub by a great storm in 1896. Then there was Studland Castle, part of Henry VIII's coastal defences. A mere blockhouse according to Gerard, it must have stood on No Man's Land, now the largest of the stacks. It was then firmly attached but became increasingly isolated until the last contact was severed, around 1920. As for the blockhouse, there are no traces. It probably fell to the sea, the one enemy it could not intimidate.

There was another Pilot's Path here, down the less-precarious north cliffs of the promontory, the pilots waiting to lead ships into Poole. The ridge and its promontory combine to shield Studland village and bay from the prevailing southwest winds. It also slows the longshore flow of sand which builds up to form the bulk of the Studland peninsula.

STUDLAND: THE BAY, THE BEACH AND THE LAKE IT ENCLOSED

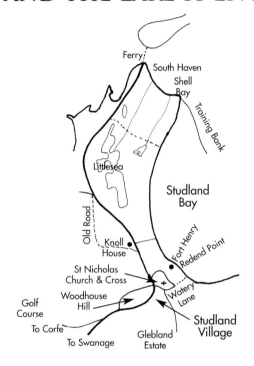

Ferry

South Haven

Shell Bay

Training Bank

Littlesea

Studland Bay

Old Road

Knoll House

Fort Henry

Redend Point

St Nicholas Church & Cross

Woodhouse Hill

Golf Course

To Corfe

To Swanage

Glebland Estate

Watery Lane

Studland Village

Denotes over 100 metres

As we grew bigger, family walks on Ballard Down ventured beyond Jardine's Seat, 'Rest and Be Thankful', past that odd suburb, Glebeland Estate, through the farmyard and down Watery Lane to the beach. So we joined the generations of kids who scratched their names into the softness of Redend Point. The yellowness of the sandstone blooms with rosy blushes and seams, giving it that name. Its surface is pock-marked with the burrows of sand wasps. Older still and alone, we passed the tilted wartime pill-box to the great sandy stretch beyond. I must have seen the large concrete bunker when exploring the thicket above the point but, with so much post-war concrete spread over Purbeck, it left no impression.

Along the great sand sweep of Studland Bay a mild wreck was an event for us. A sand dredger, the improbably-named *Sand Heap* beached northeast of Knoll House. She was one of a line, sister to the *Sand Dart* later to go ashore on St Aldhelm's Head. It must have been 1954 or 1955. My sister and I cycled over to investigate, overwhelmed by the great rusty sides rising above us. With my first camera, a plastic Kodak taking 127 film, I photographed it and the sand dunes nearby. Cameras weren't automated, and I forgot to wind on the film, so the ship appeared to sit on top of a dune. Their job made those dredgers vulnerable. A third of the team, *Sand Snipe*, later went ashore near the ferry.

The angle of the bay south of Redend Point, which was sheltered from the prevailing weather, provided a haven for passing boats including stone hackers based in Swanage. The crews were able to walk back home over the hill. The fishermen were based on that beach, and yachts still moor off-shore. It is not proof against disasters. The hurricane of 1866 whisked 14 or 15 boats sheltering there out into the Channel where they sank, taking 20 men with them. It also destroyed the rookery elms and rooks didn't breed again in Studland that century.

Trade along the Channel coast was busy, and many ships succumbed. Wrecks turned up in recent times as the craze for diving grew. A boat laden with 300 tons of stone went down just outside Poole Harbour around 1790. The crew was saved but none of the stone - not immediately, anyway. Rediscovered in the 1970s, it became known as the antler wreck, since the rest of the cargo consisted of deer antlers destined, no doubt, for the knife industry. Trev, interested in the hand-tooled Purbeck paviers of the cargo, contacted a couple of divers and we went out to retrieve some. As they were winched up I stacked each stone, knocking off and devouring the oysters. They were once an important source of food in Purbeck.

In 1984, a Spanish merchant vessel overshadowed all local wrecks. It was found when a fisherman snagged his nets off Handfast Point, and was thought, at first, to be a captured Armada vessel, which sank off Ballard whilst being towed up-Channel to Portsmouth. As fittings and cargo came to light it was clear that this wreck was a good deal earlier. Isabella polychrome ware, made in Seville, and possibly part of the cargo, helped to date this ship between 1475 and 1525. On board were stone cannonballs, a quern, one of the earliest guns found in Britain, and a pump made of birch. Only two other 16th century pumps are known. The wreck became the subject of systematic marine archaeological study, and its remnants, along with a video of their discovery, are on display in Poole Museum.

★

That Studland took off as a recherché holiday destination at the close of the 19th century was largely due to the Bankes family. Owning the village and most surrounding land, they used it as a holiday place; built villas and brought down friends. William Bankes, a friend of Byron with a fondness for guardsmen, had been exiled by Victorian hypocrisy. His brother George, who held the estate in his stead, rebuilt Studland Manor in 1848. As his son, who had been wounded in the Relief of Lucknow in 1858, lay dying, he recalled to his friends Studland summers, sailing in the bay. Poor compensation, a Victoria Cross, for his lost youth. His nephew Walter Ralph built several houses in the village including Knoll House.

Studland's beautiful, long sandy beaches and the downs, ending in chalk cliffs behind, were not yet easily accessible to trippers. The village was still a fair hike along a rough track for those who had crossed the harbour mouth in the rowed ferryboat. The road came only in preparation for the arrival of a chain ferry in 1926. An alternative was to reach Swanage by train, then hire a horse cab over the Dean Hill. That is how Viola Bankes, born in 1900, recalled it.

If the Bankes clan started a fashion, they moderated its effect. Not parting easily with land, they effectively controlled development without the intervention of planners. Only one scar resulted, Glebeland Estate, a better place to be than to see. It is a monument, they say, to a missed train. After WWI, when the glebeland came up for sale, Bankes' agent was ordered to buy. He missed the train to the auction and it passed to developers. Gradually trees are tempering its starkness.

In 1905 the Duke of Hamilton took and altered Knoll House, north of the village, for a family holiday home. The Hamiltons' arrival with their fine horses caused an annual stir in the village. Now forgotten, the once-fashionable playwright, Alfred Sutro, was amongst the first of the creative set to pick on Studland. He employed the Arts and Crafts architect Charles Voysey to build Hill Close for him. Other lesser beings followed, taking houses or cottages in the village.

After a visit in 1901 George Bernard Shaw drew it to the attention of the Bloomsbury set. In 1902 Alexander Berens, keen on Morocco and, from its inception in 1907, the Scout movement, rented and altered the house he named Full Stop (now, less imaginatively, Sandyholme). He stayed on after WWI, and founded Studland Art Industries, encouraging people to make fine leatherwork and appliqué, following techniques he had learned in the Middle East. He was influential with craft-oriented young folk of his time. Trev had a leather purse made by his aunt, who had studied with him. The sisters Vanessa and Virginia Bell (the latter to marry Leonard Woolf) holidayed here, as did Lytton Strachey, E.M. Forster, the painters Roger Fry and Duncan Grant. The Morrells had a house, too, where Lady Ottoline is supposed to have seduced Bertrand Russell. She was a Cavendish-Bentinck and cousin to George, who held Brownsea Island from 1870-91, and his son, William, who lived in Corfe's Mortons House. Even H.G. Wells must have visited. Why else would his ashes be cast on the sea off Old Harry?

Some of those early visitors settled. Sir Herbert Cook discovered Studland in 1908 and was still around thirty years later to present an organ to the church in honour of George VI's coronation. One of his daughters, Vera, married Mervyn Hamilton Fletcher and lived in the Manor House in 1939 before that too became a hotel. Later she divorced, then married Major Ryder, who had inherited the Rempstone Estate. Kenneth Anderson, founder of the Isle of Purbeck Golf Club, took over Harry Warren House, one of Walter Ralph Bankes' creations. The family has lived there ever since. Occasionally we went to parties at the house, which had a special frisson because we were told that part of raunchy *Tom Jones* was filmed there. In fact it was Michael Winner's *W11*.

During WWI the Spencer Watsons rented Corner Cottage, next to the old post office, and kept it until 1923 when, in anticipation of the ferry, they bought Dunshay. Mary recalls the excitement of the annual move down, the through train to Swanage. From there she is vague - she was little - except that those trips saw the transition from horse-drawn to motor transport. All the roads were metalled with chalk, in dry summer weather covering everything with white dust. Her thrills were the livestock, especially the twelve cart-horses at Manor Farm, where her mother's horse was stabled. As a little girl she would go to see the teams return from working the fields, watch them unharnessed, fed and watered. Both her parents continued to work: her father setting up a studio in a nearby carpenter's shop, whilst her mother bought a 20m long army hut in which to perfect mime performances. Without permission from the Bankes Estate (guessing they'd refuse), she put it up behind their house. Later it became a house.

Nothing was ever the same after the insanity of the First World War. It was followed by the threat posed to Studland's isolation by the new ferry. The Woolfs returned; Robert Graves passed by, and bohemian Augustus John would come over from his home near Poole. Maynard Keynes rented Knoll House after the Hamiltons gave up the lease in 1924, dreading the ferry. It opened as a hotel six years later, to be bought as a going concern by Col Ferguson in 1959. Purbeck's prime hotel, it has been run as a family enterprise ever since. The old track out to South Haven Point, still visible, crosses the heath behind it. The new road, part of the ferry project, runs right in front.

Suddenly Studland was on the bus route - a relaxed day out from Bournemouth or Swanage. Long an inaccessible agricultural village, it began to acquire the trappings of a seaside resort.

In some quarters, the village's new role as a fashionable retreat had a major impact. Several fishing boats worked from Studland's sheltered South Beach in the late 19th century. There were two fishing families, the Paines and the Gibbons. Soon, both saw an easier future in combining fishing with

Fishing floats; an ice lolly

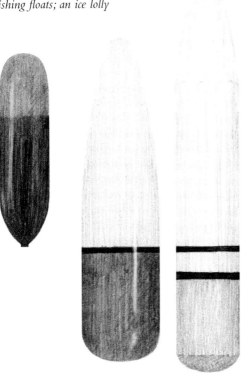

the tourist trade. Two Paine brothers, Albert and Gus, became particularly familiar with the visitors, taking them out for trips round the bay and featuring in early 20th century accounts of Studland holidays.

Fashion changed the village. It extended from a clutch of pretty stone cottages as large red brick villas marched along the Swanage road. Apart from Knoll House, the only notable secular buildings were the Manor House and a handsome barn (now gone) at the Manor Farm. The church of St Nicholas made up for this shortcoming. With St Martin's Wareham, it is the oldest church in Dorset. Its basic structure is late Saxon. Like many churches it stood on a long hallowed site. Improbably in the Victorian era, the builder W.M.Hardy protected it from threatened collapse by extensive but sensitive repair. He recorded his discoveries in a paper and in his book, *Old Swanage*. They included pre-Christian cist burials. Later, when the graveyard was extended, a Purbeck marble cist was found containing a beheaded woman and her head. A similar burial, accompanied by a 3rd century coin, was unearthed at Kimmeridge by Bernard Calkin. The reason for such decapitation, once common knowledge, is quite lost.

In the churchyard, not far from the porch, one headstone has inspired several writers. It lists the army service of Sgt Lawrence who, having taken part in many British campaigns, retired with his French wife to run a pub in Studland. A window commemorates Cornet Bankes who had so little time, fading slowly away at 21 in the vast hall of Lucknow's Bara Imambara.

Amongst the 20th century memorials is a headstone to the disinherited heir John Bankes. It bears no cross, merely 'Remember John Ralph Bankes 1937-96'. In 1983 we laid out a new gravel path there in memory of Vera Ryder. A stone seat is inscribed to a neighbour of ours, Sir Geoffrey Collins, who retired to New Swanage after a distinguished service in India and lived to be 98. Dr and Mrs Kennett lie here, too. He was known in Purbeck as a capable and popular doctor. I remember walking into his large surgery and, even before approaching his desk to outline my symptoms, he looked up over half-moon reading glasses to ask, 'How long have you had yellow jaundice?' They died in a road accident in France in 1984. The three girls were friends of ours, living just down the road in Shore House. As one gets older cemeteries are no longer hostile: gradually they fill with friends.

It is a pretty little church, more twelfth century than Saxon, with rounded Norman arches and a squat, pent-roofed tower. The carved corbels above the north and south walls are particularly attractive - not just the couple copulating inconspicuously by the peak of the porch roof. They are like the erotica in Indian murals - unnoticed by passers-by but familiar to all the 16-year-olds. Most bear human heads, singly or in twos, but there are donkeys' and boars' heads, a horse in harness and geometric shapes. As to the rest, the guidebook is better on the ancient than the modern.

On a little mound beside the road up to the church stands a circular worked piece of heathstone some 1.2 m in diameter and 50cm high. A rectangular socket at its centre probably held the stem of a wooden or stone cross. In the mid-1970s someone suggested commissioning a new cross. The rector approached Treleven Haysom, who offered to charge only for the stone. He carved that cross to satisfy himself, neither for God nor Mammon, but turned to many Celtic and Saxon crosses for decorative motifs, the archer and the vine of life. With them he integrated modern elements: a violin, Concorde, the Bomb that overshadowed our youth. The line in runes he drew from *Bhagavadgita*, a discourse in the vast Hindu epic, *Mahabharata*. Misquoted ever since, it says simply 'I am what I eat and I eat what I am'.

Watery Lane leads down from the cross mound, curving north near the track to Old Harry and down to the beach, passing below the Bankes Arms, now a busy, popular pub. The lane itself continues beside a stream to South Beach, where the fishermen were based.

The Second World War closed the tourist trade. The Studland peninsula was taken over by the military and the navy shelled the northern section. A controlled area, restrictions were imposed on the residents who were not even supposed to glance seawards. It became particularly important in the lead-up to the Normandy landings. In 1943 Canadian engineers built Fort Henry above Redend Point, a massive bunker with a slit observation window 30m long across its face to give VIPs a wonderful, safe view of trial landings. Beside it was a gun battery. Too much of a challenge to demolish after the war it was left, overgrown. Now cleaned up, it has become 'heritage'. From here George VI and Winston Churchill watched a major exercise, 'Smash', a prelude to the D-Day landings two months later.

Extending our known world along the beach towards the ferry, it was the mid-fifties when we started to explore Littlesea. The war was over barely ten years and the area had been heavily bombarded. A team of Poles had removed 84,000 missiles and 200 unexploded bombs but it was still richly scattered with rusty ammunition, some coloured red or green. We stayed clear of suspicious things, examining without touching.

There were other hazards. I fell through the ice on a couple of occasions, only to cycle home with flooded boots. Inspired by a book on fishing, I spent a day beside the lake hoping for a bass, the author having declared there was no better place to catch them than Littlesea. It was a lesson in the fallibility of the printed word. The only fish in the lake – eels and thirteen-spined sticklebacks – were not enticed by my ragworm. There was an attempt to introduce trout in the 1930s, but they didn't survive shelling or the hostile environment.

In 1958 we put a raft on Littlesea. I was never a craftsman. Robert and Richard built it at Ulwell Farm, using a door and a frame holding eight oil drums. They were architects, not explorers. Once it was on the lake I used it most, pushing through the reeds from one stretch of water to the next. No one interfered. Rare marsh harriers nested there then – the sort of secret information kids weren't supposed to know. When we told earnest, expert birders they put us down. Not realising that we were deemed too young to be trusted, we thought them blind since the birds passed food for the chicks to one another in full sight of the road.

That Capt Cyril Diver chose to study the ecology of Studland Heath in the 1930s must have had a considerable bearing on its future. He became the first Director General of the Nature Conservancy in 1948. In 1962 it leased 1500 acres (later extended) of the heath, including Littlesea, from the Bankes estate. I shared a flat on Brownsea with the warden of the new reserve, Bunny Teagle and his wife, Joyce. He mentioned an odd frame with rusty tins he had found abandoned at the edge of the lake. That's where we'd left the raft, leaking badly, after a last hazardous voyage down the lake. In saving one environment, another is destroyed. Today the east shore of the lake looks stark, partially cleared of vegetation. There is a fenced Heather Walk and where the raft lay stands a smart new hide. No. 4, it is labelled, to avoid confusion with No. 2 and No. 7. Is there no place for kids like us any more?

Littlesea is, as lakes go, very new. Old maps show the shore of Studland Bay well back towards the Ferry Road, an uneven coastline, not the smooth modern sweep. That is what Gerard describes: 'Then come wee to a longe crooked Land, named South Haven Poynt, for that it defendeth the South Side of the Haven of Poole...' The coast he knew still exists as the western shore of Littlesea. Longshore drift created a sand spit which gradually short-cut the old coastline and wind blew the dry sand into dune ridges. The enclosed lagoon was fed by acid heath streams until all trace of salt vanished. The modern lake, tinted rust by the peat, is very shallow. Having punted and swum over most of it, I know that little is out of my depth. Its water is not rich in life, nevertheless duck come here in winter. Mallard and teal stay to nest. Cormorants and herons make a bid for the eels. There used to be a huge starling roost amongst the reeds. In evening, cycling back from the ferry, we ran the gauntlet of these tight smoke-like flocks, droppings pattering across the tarmac like heavy rain as they passed.

They say that Shell Bay, at the far end of the peninsula, acquired its name in the 1900s from the old ferrymen, an inducement to tourists from the far shore. As the sand advanced to create the smooth curve of Studland Bay, then turned towards the harbour mouth to build up this further arc, Littlesea's exit to the sea was pushed ever northwards. Today each of two brown streams draining it open here after passing through boggy sallow thickets graced with elegant royal fern.

Shell Bay had a narrow escape. In 1923 the Spencer Watsons went to Kingston Lacy to attend the inauguration of Ralph Bankes as new landlord. He had inherited aged two, but this was his coming-of-age. There they saw extensive plans for a development on the lines of Sandbanks. Without parting with any land, they could have made a killing. No doubt overruling accountants and solicitors, Bankes scrapped the plans. History may prove the old land-owning families to be wiser, better administrators than The National Trust that has taken their place. At their best they have at stake honour, responsibility to families who have been their tenants for generations, and a pride and love for the land they have inherited. But, to be fair, whoever rules creates an opposition.

As long as I can remember the north end of Studland Beach had both a 'gay' and a nudist tendency. Perhaps the nudism stemmed from the Duke of Hamilton's clan who earned a reputation for strolling the beach naked. Now it has been formalised with signs. Sadly, it is no place to see Greek sculptures in the flesh. There are exceptions. One day, walking back to the road along the northern track in the late afternoon, I found myself behind two bronzed apollos in swimming trunks. At the main road they stopped expectantly...and a police car turned up. Plain-unclothed policemen!

Dividing the two bays is the Training Bank, a great breakwater of un-shaped rock constructed to train the current to drop its sand and silt away from the main channel. A huge project, it was begun in the late 19th century. Later much of the stone rock was carried in empty clay trains to Goathorn Pier then shipped here. It was not completed until 1927.

There has been a succession of refreshment places at South Haven Point. The present fish restaurant, Shell Bay, with its good reputation for food, if not for architecture, follows a café. Before that there was an inn, already derelict in 1880, where people could wait for the ferryman to row over.

The Ferry Road carried a toll even for bicycles. In 1992 the company took a step too far in gravelling the verges and setting up parking meters for the many vehicles that stop at either side. Somehow they contravened the law and soon the meters disappeared.

That road and the western fringe of the village itself form a vague border between Studland and its bay and the barren heathland stretching westward to the far border of Purbeck. Once the land of the poor, the fuzz-croppers, today it is the source of Purbeck's greatest wealth.

THE HEATH:
EAST OF WAREHAM ROAD

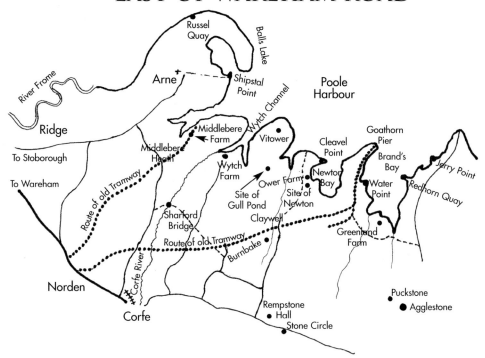

Taking the bus to Bournemouth with my mother, I was fascinated by the view to the left as the road descended towards the pines of Woodhouse Hill. There lay a fresh landscape, heather and russet bracken so different from the green valley which was home. Widening my horizons, that heath was an obvious draw. Bobby Bingham, who lived down the road, knew a place among the trees on the far side of the Golf Course where people illicitly dumped rubbish. It was the sort of stuff left in inherited houses, judged as not worth the effort to sort and sell. For us it was treasure. We rooted amongst it, turning up Chinese porcelain incense burners, a silver turnip watch, a silver skull for storing matches, brass optical instruments, white balloons my mother turned straight out. (No, they weren't contraceptives, but they were certainly medical). In spring those little daffodils they call Lent Lilies graced the place.

That rich seam exhausted, we moved out into the heath, down the ridge to great anvil-shaped Agglestone. There are many explanations for its name. I choose Saxon 'halig' (holy) stone with no more justification than those who prefer 'hagge' (witch), 'hagol' (hail) or Egglestan (sharp, upsticking stone). Everyone has a different tale as to its origin, too. Prior to 19th century scientific advances it was deep mystery and most tales involved the devil up to mischief, hurling the rock from France. I was told he was aiming at Salisbury Cathedral, as it rose to the glory of God. In a more secular age Corfe Castle has become the target. That, too, would be passing diabolical. They agree more happily on Puckstone, lost in gorse some 200 metres to the northwest. Puck, the imp, was responsible. Nobody claims it was thrown anywhere, but it is small and insignificant. Developments in geology provided a prosaic answer. Both were made of particularly resilient deposits of grit from the Bagshot beds, which resisted erosion as it wore down the softer material around.

Agglestone earned a significance all of its own when an unpopular schoolmaster, taking a group of pupils for a walk, showed his agility by climbing to its top. He then couldn't get down. The rock was never the same again to any grammar school kid. Then it shifted. Some say it was 1970, or that it happened gradually. I just remember going one day and a handsome anvil silhouette was replaced by the present tilted aberration.

The bog in the foot of the valley on either side of Agglestone breeds marsh orchids, yellow bog asphodel, cotton grass and deep blue marsh gentians. Dartford warblers, mascot of this heathland, creep amongst the gorse or perch on a sprig to sing a jingly snatch of song. At the extremity of their range, they are vulnerable to cold winters. The naturalist Mansel-Pleydell thought them wiped out by the harsh winters of the 1880s. The 1963 cold spell reduced them to 11 pairs nationwide. Each time they just survive. At present they flourish, even invading the gorse of the chalk ridge.

There are streamlets down through the mossy bog in each valley of that patch of heathland. Some opened into long, deep pools over white sand where on hot days I stopped to bathe. The water flows more slowly now and they have become grubby depths. Conifer plantations, soon populated by large wood ants' nests, were advancing onto the heath when we first went there. In the early fifties 1500 acres were planted on this part of Purbeck. Meanwhile a patch of heavily-fertilised grassland began to eat southwards into the heather from Greenland Farm. The heath retreated.

Exploring ever westwards we passed Rempstone Hall and the copse sheltering an ancient stone circle. That was magic from the first day I set eyes on it because four brand new tennis balls floated mysteriously in an adjoining pond. The stones are shapeless lumps of that same gritty ironstone. Perhaps once set up more impressively and not lost in trees, they have become unremarkable. Recently, with the demise of god, people have turned back to such things for spiritual comfort. An occasional candle burns there and feathers or odd-shaped pebbles perch on a stone. In little niches coins are stowed to pleasure the pixies.

Don't knock the pixies! I'll tell you a recent story. I dropped by to show the stone circle to some friends and noticed those coins, as they nosed around. Being practical (and always short of cash) I quietly pocketed them, reasoning that it was a favour to all concerned. The pixies didn't feature (well, I ask you!); the donors would find their coins gone, and be pleased that the pixies did feature, and I had over half a pint of bitter.

Soon afterwards I flew into Delhi, carrying a lot of cash to buy the motorcycle Pete and I planned to drive home. Through a series of the oddest coincidences £200, made up of four pretty red notes, were pinched from my bag by my friend's fourteen year old servant. The boy swore he hadn't touched it (nor the pretty sweeties, nor the big bar of chocolate). There was no one else - no one mortal. Nothing like that had ever happened to me before. Months later, back in Purbeck, I returned the pixies' money with interest. Why look for trouble?

Rempstone Hall, set back from the road near the stone circle, had been bought as a farmhouse by John Calcraft in 1757 then improved to a worthy residence. Calcraft gathered a considerable estate, including Wareham, during the late 18th century. Old Mrs Calcraft, the formidable squire when Mrs Panton arrived as a new bride, left the estate to her grandson, Capt Marston. With little emotional tie to the place, he presided over the sale of Worth. Mrs Panton also mentions that he burned many priceless family papers but he sued her for libel. He won £250 damages and her book was suppressed. A hand-written note in the Smedmore copy of her book records that the Captain told the writer he had burned a lot of old rubbish including 'odd bits of paper'. From him the estate passed to the Ryder family.

Beyond Rempstone we followed the road descending past Burnbake towards Ower. I knew Burnbake from earlier times, calling it 'Burnbrake' until very recently when someone pointed out the error. Friends of my mother's lived at Burnbake Cottage when I was about ten. Their son was a contemporary of mine, so I stayed there occasionally. The only sharp memory is of my first birth, in the shape of their their goat having a kid, and I arriving at the final moment. I remember the bluish colour of the translucent membrane covering the struggling new life, and the smell of the goat's warm fur, if you stuck your nose against it.

The track led on to Newton Bay, an inlet of Poole Harbour which became a favourite outing. The bay was either full of water with shelduck leading ducklings in summer, or an expanse of shining mud echoing to the calls of curlew and redshank. We ate our sandwiches there in a low oak tree, looking across to Ower, from where the mediaeval marble was exported – not that we knew anything of its history then.

Newton Bay was named for its new town, founded under Edward I in 1286. It was to have a twice-weekly market and an annual fair. By monopolising the busy marble trade, then reaching its peak, it should have rivalled Poole, which had got its charter as a port in 1248. It failed and disappeared without trace. We thought it lay beneath the mossy banks which ran through the woods at the base of Goathorn. The actual site was almost certainly discovered during the BP archaeological survey prior to launching operations in the area. Whilst everyone assumed it was southeast of Newton Bay, a BP aerial survey revealed the outline of a settlement in the most logical place – just southwest. It stood astride the route to Ower, poised to exploit and expand on that principal marble port. Excavations produced very few artefacts and it seems likely that, having been set out under royal orders, the town was never actually settled. It is remarkable that no permanent village grew up at Ower, given the size of the marble trade over a long period.

For us kids, Brands Bay came later. Was it the following winter? Time moved so slowly, in those days. The cold weather brought many birds, and there were a couple of large, unexplained wrecks abandoned on the shore to inspire thoughts of drama. Then as now inverted dinghies (tenders for boats moored in the deep channel) lay on Redhorn Point. Along the shore from Redhorn is Jerry Point. I always assumed that to be a recent name but Treswell's map of 1586 shows it as Gerie Orde. The suffix was applied elsewhere and when in 1852 the Admiralty gave permission for a landing place at Goathorn the name given was Goat Orde Point. The dictionary gives 'ord' as 'a point'.

On the west side of the Ferry Road is a rough turning. Enticed, we followed it until we reached that Goathorn pier. There is a little bay on the east shore of Goathorn, sheltered by the high sweet chestnut trees of Water Point. We christened it Curlew Cove, never dreaming that the mast of an oil well would rise a couple of hundred metres away. In November 1956, while working out another route to Goathorn to avoid the Ferry Road toll, 'we crossed the little, old railway long since pulled up...' not realising that the track beside Curlew Cove was part of the same rail-less tramway. An embankment remained between it and harbour, concealing us from birds on the water or mud.

The track from the Ferry road to Curlew Cove, then as now running over wartime steel, passed Newton Heath's extensive clay diggings. Mains electricity was yet to arrive and 'all the houses around here have small windpumps for water, which also generate electricity when necessary. They are on poles like those of telegraph lines'. That diary entry from February

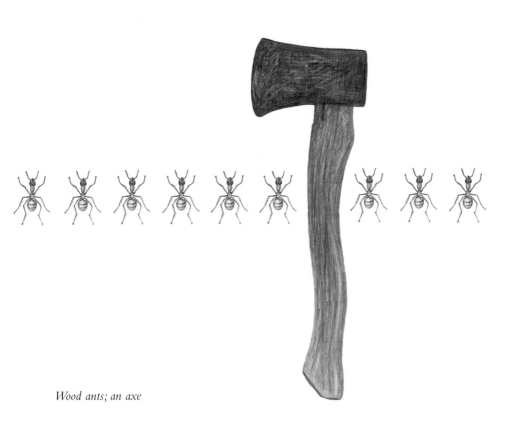

Wood ants; an axe

1956 includes a drawing labelled 'water mill'. They were merely generators, of course, similar to that still operating at Bonvils near Worth. Probably 'the man in the caravan' had told us that the propeller made the electricity to work the pump, and I'd got it slightly wrong! There were several ruined buildings, victims of wartime naval shelling, and near them a caravan. 'The man in the caravan' features several times in my 1956 diary. He was Philip Warner, brother to the Warners of Langton's Spyway School. Having returned from Tasmania he was overseeing reconstruction of a ruined cottage and planned to settle there with his family. He was friendly and seemed quite glad of us kids disturbing his peace. His eldest son Nick lives there now.

His cottage was the old school house intended for clay workers' children. The tramway ran so close that a lean-to against the end-wall housed the engine at night. A couple of photographs on the wall, taken around 1900, show some 30 pupils gathered around their teacher. When an extension to Corfe opened in 1905 the school was doomed and, before long, the train carried kids to school there. The clayworkers' cottages, destroyed during the second world war, are lost in undergrowth. The carpenter's shed and part of a clay-drying shed remain. Both are built of clay bound with heather beneath a coat of bitumen. There was even a corrugated iron chapel nearby.

Climate and drainage were very different when the Bagshot Beds were laid down. Water from the highlands of Dartmoor poured through the Poole Basin towards the Solent river, depositing quartz pebbles and sand or, when flowing more gently, the pure white slurry of decayed feldspar. Both derived from those granite hills. The quartz pieces, consolidated in an iron-rich cement, formed the sand and grit layers of the Beds. Rotten feldspar formed its lenses of fine clay. There are two main clay seams: one running near the chalk ridge from Povington through Creech, Norden and Rempstone; the other, lower in the basin, from East Holme through Ridge and Claywell to Newton. The two contrasting sediments show in the bank of Brands Bay's shore: the sands near Redhorn Quay, and the clay at Jerry Point.

Successive settlers in Purbeck were not slow to appreciate its clay. Potteries and kilns were set up on the heath from prehistoric times. Most pottery unearthed at Maiden Castle was of Purbeck clay. The Romans soon adopted it, and the Second Legion was using Purbeck pottery for all its coarse ware. Known to archaeologists as Black Burnished Ware, and made without a wheel, it comprises more than half the coarse pottery found at Hadrian's Wall. Soon Purbeck's potters were producing Roman forms for their new clients.

In the 17th century there was a demand for cups and mugs. When those long, elegant, frequently-broken tobacco pipes became fashionable, the deposit became known as Pipe Clay. Why it was later called Ball Clay is less certain. The Industrial Revolution caused a dramatic surge in demand. Josiah Wedgwood needed 1400 tons each year. In 1771 Thomas Hyde, his family already a century in the clay business, agreed to provide it from Arne. He shipped it to Poole from his own Hyde Quay, and there it was loaded onto sea-going vessels, a pattern which persisted until the late 19th century. An Italian marble tablet in Arne church commemorates his passing. Demand soared and two centuries of exploitation have transformed the heathland scenery.

As unquestioning boys we crossed and recrossed derelict clay tramway embankments whilst exploring the heath. We traced the harbour coast too, sinking through superficial grey mud into the stinking black filth beneath, flooding boots. People told us of black-headed gulls nesting at a Gull Pond somewhere on the heath. Joan Begbie wrote in the 1930s of being pursued there by angry gulls. No map marked it. It took some time to accept that the gull-less boggy patch we found had been famous for its gulls. Patterns change. Spartina grass spreading out into the mud flats provided the gulls with a safer place to lay their very-edible eggs. We found them nesting in spartina at Arne when we went there on a failed mission to trace a heronry said to have thrived before the war.

Used as a decoy for Holton Heath's cordite factory, Arne was battered during WWII. Lights and flares here and on Brownsea Island attracted heavy German bombing. Things were recovering in the fifties and there was a little car-park with an honesty box beside the school house. Honesty, too, covered the sales of fizzy drinks. It never occurred to us to take a bottle of horrid-red cherryade without putting 6d in the open box and we rarely had 6d.

The church opposite was built in the early 13th century and includes Stoborough in its parish. In 1643 the Parliamentarians burned Stoborough to deny the royalists a base from which to attack Wareham. None of its buildings predate 1700 but it retained a mayor until 1714. King's Barrow, the greatest monument there, was cut through during the making of the turnpike road to Creech. At its centre was a hollow oak trunk 3m long and 1.2m in diameter. It held the burnt bones of a man wrapped in deerskin, and sewn up along with some golden wire and an ornamented basin of oak wood.

The heath is always vulnerable to fire. Each summer the fire engine's bell clanging up Ulwell Road past our house would draw attention to smoke rising behind the chalk ridge. Sometimes we followed the trail of water-splashes along the road to watch a heath blaze, which might be enlivened by explosions as the flames caught leftover munitions. In April 1974 Trev and I were in his boat off St Aldhelm's Head when fragments of ash fell from the sky. We landed and drove to the fire, joining other men beating back the flames. As darkness fell an orange line of fire advanced slowly across the heath from Agglestone to the golf course. Gradually we won but it was 1am before we left. A slight breeze would soon rekindle the flames. After each fire the bare, black land seemed hopeless, but different plants re-established themselves remarkably quickly, and following a predictable sequence.

Looking from Littlesea on New Year's Day 1974, I saw '...a sudden cloud of smoke in the west and later discovered that the drillers have struck oil at Wytch'. Wytch Farm soon became the most productive onshore field in Western Europe. At first they were drawing oil from Bridport sandstone 900m below Poole Harbour. They separated water, gas and oil at Wytch before sending the oil by pipeline to a rail terminal at Furzebrook. In 1978 a larger reservoir was found at a depth of 1,600m in Sherwood sandstone. By the mid-eighties 60,000 barrels a day were flowing from here by pipeline to a terminal by Southampton Water. Despite early opposition from drivers who prefer not to see oil extraction, this lucrative industry is remarkably unobtrusive.

We knew Wytch long before oil was found. Close to the nucleus of the modern oilfield, at the mouth of Corfe River, Middlebere and Wytch Lakes, which are creeks rather than ponds, were good for birds. Other folk saw spoonbills there. I had to be content with harriers, great flocks of wintering black-tailed godwits and duck. Sometimes we followed up the river, or even traced it down from Corfe to its mouth. In summer this entailed a battle with undergrowth, brambles, nettles and the like. The route took us near Scotland Farm. From there a footpath runs westward to cross the river by a small bridge of finely-worked stone. This held the sluices to flood the neighbouring watermeadows. It is older than it looks, bearing the date 1711 and the neatly inscribed initials of William Ockden (related by marriage to the prominent Uvedales of Corfe) and the current Nathaniel Bond. Further downstream a bridleway crosses the river by little stone Sharford Bridge, its parapet disfigured in 1980 by cocks'n'hens, the upright stones that top walls. The name features on early maps, before roads were included, as the only easy crossing of this tiny river. Nearby masonry remains from the 18th century sluices, which once flooded the surrounding meadows.

The Corfe river runs into Wytch Lake, one finger of the vast estuary of Poole Harbour. The shoreline is hopelessly uneven. Points of harder, higher land interdigitate with shining waters and shining mud. Harder and higher tracts, cut off amongst those waters and mud, rise as islands.

THE HARBOUR AND THE ISLANDS

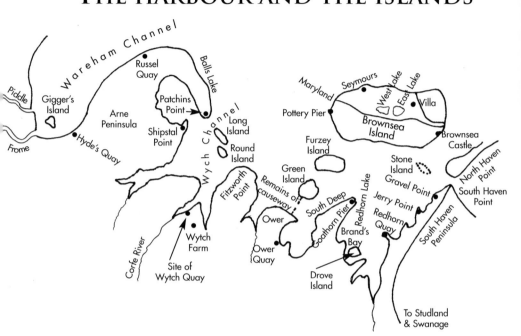

South Haven Peninsula combines with North Haven to form the gateway of Poole Harbour. Only a 400m wide channel flows between them. The tidal rush of water through the narrow entrance has scoured out its bed until it is almost 20 metres deep in places. Through these gates the surprising bulk of the cross-Channel ferry and other smaller vessels glide and turn northwards to follow the main channel into Poole. The great estuary calms the rivers which feed it, causing their waters to drop a burden of sediment to build up the flats of fine grey silt. They create the harbour's shining low tide landscape. We soon learnt how deep that mud could be, and that the grey surface concealed stinking black ooze.

The low-tide mudscape is cut by steep-sided channels carrying the main body of river and tidal flow. Like the twigs of some great tree, fine networks of runnels join as branches; great boughs then run into the trunk, that main channel passing to the sea. All that is solid in this softness is the channel bed where the heavier sediment falls. For the rest, the flats are more lethal than water. To those who fish or shoot over it, each branch has a name. Posts mark the channels, and, at night, lights line the main deep to Poole.

Before the train reached Wareham in 1847 water provided the main approach to Purbeck. That Turner came by water in 1811 is suggested by two of the paintings that resulted. One shows the view towards the ridge and Corfe from Poole's Constitution Hill, the other a near view of the castle.

White describes the journey: 'From Poole to Wych Passage – the usual landing place for Corfe – the distance is about seven miles, and the boatmen lounging on the quay are always ready to take you there on their own terms "T'was too much of a pull for one," said the weatherbeaten old fellow, "besides meeting the tide coming back." He would, however, take three shillings, and I agreeing, he hailed another of his own genus, as rugged as himself to pull the second oar, and away we went...'

White and the men talk as they row: about the decline of trade, how it had ceased with Newfoundland, and the low numbers of salmon. Another grievance is that since the opening of the railway so few persons go to the castle by water. They prefer to travel down the line to Wareham, four miles from Corfe, and there take the omnibus. They turn into Ball's Lake – 'lake' here being the local term for a passage connecting two channels.

'And presently we were in Wych Channel, a narrow water-course, twisting in innumerable curves between the slimy banks...a pile or a bush fixed at the bends, to mark the channel at high water. Still narrower grows the channel, leaving scarcely room for the oars; at last a house surrounded by trees appears to the left, and a little wharf, to which is moored a sloop laden with coals...' White puzzles how that managed to get there, then sets off for Corfe. 'A few yards along the rough track leading from the landing place and you are on Wych Heath, a breezy wilderness of furze and bracken, the very spot for starting a day's walk with gladsome feeling. I slung on my knapsack, and bent my steps towards the ruin...'

The painter Turner would have followed exactly the same route in 1811. Then aged 36 he probably walked too, with the special knapsack he had designed to hold his sketching gear.

Not only the usual way for visitors to come to the castle, the Wytch boat carried Corfe folk to and from Poole's market. There were the inevitable accidents. Hutchins talks of one in March 1759, when the market boat from Poole was blown onto the mudflats. Of the 19 passengers on board 'many of them in liquor', thirteen tried to wade to Brownsea Island; all sank in the mud and were drowned. The remaining six were saved by another boat. Such drownings happened at regular, if long, intervals so it was hardly surprising that the Corfe folk were quick to take advantage of the train.

There were other portlets: Russel Quay, at the end of the Arne peninsula was busy with Wareham traffic; Redhorn Quay, projecting to Redhorn Lake, the deep channel in Brands Bay, was the main route from Swanage and Studland to Poole. The cliffstone foundation of the stone hard (to Robinson a 'rude banker') running parallel to the channel survives. There was night traffic. At the height of smuggling in the 18th and early 19th centuries, the isolated rugged coast of Purbeck was excellent for landing contraband. Once landed it had to reach its market. The main route through Wareham was well patrolled, as was the mouth of the harbour. The complex coast of the estuary was harder to control. Smuggled goods was carried to such little jetties to be rowed through the familiar channels to Poole. When using Redhorn they rowed the long way west of Brownsea to avoid excise men near the harbour mouth. Once in Poole the cargo was hard to trace.

Smuggling will always continue, only the contraband varies. It was still wine and spirits when in April 1947 a group of men, including an ex-naval officer, loaded a ship at Cherbourg. Transferring their cargo to a landing craft off the Isle of Wight, they cruised right across the harbour to Shipstal Point on the Arne peninsula. There they shifted the booty onto a lorry and set off, but someone in that then almost derelict village questioned the police about this night-time lorry. Each ended up in jail and there was a heavy fine. Today only drugs or migrants provide a sufficient mark-up to justify the risk.

Redhorn was the last ferry from the south shore to Poole. The train didn't reach Swanage until 1885. Even then the boat was more convenient for Studland folk. Prior to the turn of that century, Sandbanks was not a major settlement, and the rowing boat crossing the harbour mouth was less important than that running into Poole.

Poole Harbour sustained legal commerce from very early times. Excavations reveal the rise and fall of several ports, evidence of overseas trade from the last centuries BC. By the end of the 1st century AD, the estuary may have displaced Hengistbury Head as the most important cross-channel trading area on Britain's south coast. The Romans certainly exploited it, setting up a harbour at Hamworthy during Vespasian's invasion of 43 AD. One of the four legions involved landed supplies here and built a road to their fortress at modern Lake Farm, north of Poole. If these sites are outside, Roman influence did not bypass Purbeck.

Wareham was prominent as a Saxon port but in later mediaeval times silting of the Frome boosted rival Poole. Ower, as the main outlet for a flood of mediaeval worked Purbeck marble, still receives its token passage-fee from the marblers. Probably the marble quay was at Cleavel Point where the modern deep channel flows closest to the shore.

Cleavel Point has a longer history. Hutchins mentions a submerged bridge from there to Green Island. It was built around 200BC, timber piles retaining a matrix of clay, sand and rubble interspersed with layers of brushwood with an upper surface of Purbeck stone slabs. The huge quantity of stone involved was probably ferried from Peveril Point.

Was it a causeway running to a bridge or two opposing jetties, the basis of an Iron-Age port? That the two structures are slightly out of alignment and there is no trace of piles to support a bridge between them is cited as evidence for a port. But an error in alignment could be accidental and traces of any bridge structure might not survive two millennia in the migratory deep channel. A bridge to the dual island (Furzey and Green Islands then one) doesn't preclude the port. The Green Island section, site of a settlement, thrived on manufacturing shale, clay and iron goods. BP's archaeological survey in the early 1980s also revealed that a Bronze Age presence was followed by the construction of an earthwork enclosure some seventy metres square in the south east of Furzey. There are minor boundaries, too, and traces of intensive agriculture. The settlement was abandoned towards the end of the 1st century BC, probably in favour of Ower. While active, it traded with Gaul either directly or through the port at Hengistbury. In 1964 an Iron Age dugout was dredged up off Brownsea, and ten years later Alan Bromby discovered traces of a Roman settlement 70m out from the island, evidence that the sea level had fallen some 2m in the interim. Foreign trade from the Purbeck coast of the harbour continued into the 20th century, clay still being loaded onto sailing vessels at Goathorn in the 1920s.

The harbour was a winter draw for us boys. In spring and summer, the cliff coast was more attractive, with all its colonial sea birds, along with the swimming and climbing. The harbour supported a less-concentrated breeding population, and was less generous in its excitements. With winter, all manner of Arctic birds begin to swing in onto the mudflats. The mud is rich in the invertebrate life they seek. There were few geese then. Semi-wild Canadas had not settled, and Brent geese, now plentiful, were scarce but the masses of duck were hunted from land and water. Punt gunners, lying low, a heavy gun at the bow, negotiated spartina-lined channels hoping to surprise some feeding flock. Feigning innocence, we would casually put up the prey. There were waders, too, who became a smoke of little birds moving in magic harmony: now sharp white, now vanished dark, as every bird turned together. Rarities appeared and were argued over.

Many marine ducks including scoter, eider, long-tailed duck, goosander, red-breasted merganser, cormorants, divers and grebes roost on the sea, and feed in the harbour, commuting morning and night through the harbour entrance. Cycling out before dawn, we counted them in or, at dusk, out.

A common interest in birds crossed age barriers. Amongst others we would meet was Helen Brotherton, who has played such a major role in conserving Dorset's environment. We exchanged news, news that might send the recipient on an unexpected chase. Then came a familiar catastrophe: oil

A sprig of Scots Pine;
the oakleaf emblem of The National Trust

pollution. The accident happened inside the harbour in late January 1961, when it was full of birds. Two ships, one Soviet, collided, spilling a mass of oil. Immediately the shore was littered with oiled birds, dead and living. We caught what we could. In our warm kitchen my mother tolerated two guillemots, two black-necked grebes, a great northern diver and a little purple sandpiper. Part of an organised survey, we patrolled the shore, marking each dead beak with red nail polish to avoid double counting.

There had been human disasters, too. Folk told of a wartime pilot who had baled out and landed in the mud never to be seen again. Flying boats crashed during the war, too. The worst accident happened when an RAF Catalina hit Round Island whilst landing in mist. Regular flights from Southampton had been shifted 'for the duration' to less-threatened Poole Harbour. At Foynes, in Eire, one could connect with a Pan Am flight to the States. With other army officers, my father flew from Poole Yacht Club in June 1943. To pass through two neutral countries they posed as civilians, each wearing the same overcoat over his uniform for the appropriate passport photograph. At Foynes they waited for darkness to continue to Lisbon since the previous daytime flight had been shot down. Theirs was a devious route via Lagos, where they changed to a Sunderland to continue up the Congo, down the Nile to Cairo and on to Palestine, still a free Arab land.

Flying-boats were abandoned for passenger transport soon after the war but a line of three or four moored off Hamworthy delighted every passing child. Then they were no longer there. It seems the last were broken up in 1959.

My first job, through the freeze-up of early 1963, entailed sweeping floors and smashing flawed glass apparatus in Poole. An unsent letter: 'You should see Poole Harbour - thick ice. Our factory is on West Quay and I make all possible excuses to get out onto the quay. It really looks lovely. The sky is always frost-clear. There are little boats with beautiful reflections in the calm water, and huge sheets of ice flowing in the direction of the tide.'

Dissatisfied with commuting, I applied for the post of assistant warden-naturalist of the then-Dorset Naturalists' Trust reserve on Brownsea Island. I got the job. When the owner, reclusive Mrs Bonham-Christie, died in 1961, her grandson gave the island to the Treasury in lieu of death duties. It passed to The National Trust. He kept a house by the quay and an ancient Morris car. (There had been two cars. I helped put the wreck of the other into Poole Harbour for a mooring.) The DNT leased the north section of the island. The National Trust retained the south, with Alan Bromby as their warden. He was interested in moths, showing me how to trap them with a light. The John Lewis Partnership bought the Castle. Originally built as a defensive blockhouse under Henry VIII, it had played a role in the defence of Parliamentary Poole in 1642-43.

Col Waugh, who owned the island from 1852 to 1856, tried to exploit its clay. Dreaming of porcelain, he ended up with sanitary ware, and failed to meet his creditors. There were shafts up to 22m deep at Seymours, on the northwest of the island, and a tramway carried the clay to a factory by the southwest coast. George Cavendish Bentinck took over in 1870, staying at the Vicarage which he renamed The Villa. His household included his wife, daughter Venetia and a staff of eleven. By April I was installed in The Villa's ground floor. Upstairs lived the Warden, Mr Walton and his wife. The ground floor was eerie and neglected. 'I hardly dare to wander into the dark corridors smelling of damp and decay. It is still rather exciting - a pity that that has to wear off.'

The bay window of my room looked out onto a marsh past an elegant birch tree. On the second day a marsh harrier carrying nest material landed amongst the reeds just in front. The huge stone-flagged kitchen looked darkly into pine wood, where fifty pairs of nesting herons made odd, alarming noises. The rats were alarming, too, welcoming tenants, careless with food. Six years earlier, the island had been officially declared rat-free. Later I had company. Bunny and Joyce Teagle took part of the ground floor, he being the warden of the new Studland Nature Reserve and both were excellent naturalists. Joyce excelled in the kitchen, too. So, I deferred to her there, while Bunny showed me how to live-trap and identify small mammals.

At first I had to work a hand-pump each day to fill the tank in the roof with yellowish water before walking to the quay to meet the postman and collect our bread, milk and post. Even then his was the only daily boat delivery in the country. The rest of the day was spent on tasks like clearing rhododendrons, which infested much of the island. We started with Venetia Park, set out in the late 19th century, and named after that same daughter. The ornamental plants were gone, save for bamboo and a single scarlet rhododendron among so many mauve. Walls and gravel tracks emerged as we advanced. The bamboo was turned into screens beside the walled lagoon (a failed reclamation scheme by Col Waugh) and the two lakes.

I was also delegated to keep a watch for egg collectors at the black-headed gull colony: 'Got up at 4am, had breakfast, and was out by the Gullery by 4.30. It was still very dark but the birds already sang. The few boats in the harbour carried riding lights. It was calm and the tide low - the moon made everything grey. Shelduck quacked on the mud over the sea wall, and the gulls were yelling. No one came but I sat patiently until after 6am. Then I walked along the north shore...' They never did come. The only intruders onto the island's mudflats were men digging for cockles or ragworm.

After Lady Baden Powell opened Brownsea in mid-May, I took twice-daily tours around the sanctuary. On 2nd June, taking a group '... down to The Villa...saw smoke, dark to the southwest... I ran through the archway along Middle Street; on up the south firebreak through gorse towards the smoke. Got to where the firebreak was being widened in the very face of the fire. Took a beater from a nearby scout, and beat at the flames until, bit by bit we extinguished the north part of the fire, and we worked west and southwest along it. Heat, thick smoke, we beat, cough, eyes water and sting, shirts scorch, faces shielded, sweat. A northeast wind blows smoke over us, the red sun through the pall, the scouts working well... the water glittering red through the trees and smoke, like more fire. Burning beater - rubber smell. The fire's last struggle held at a steep piece of coast as we tried to keep it back from more gorse... flames at the bottom raged up, and undid all our work at the top. The fire rallied and spread again uphill, branches and pine needles caught and became torches, unbearable heat. Three or four of us caught in the middle of the flames, semi-panic... Every so often, a miniature tornado of hot black smoke flew at us. We choked and struggled out. The whole thing started to collapse - less flame, less heat. Hoses up from a landing craft...'

The fire was the only time I went in the Bonham-Christies' Morris. I was given a lift home in its boot. It burned a large part of the southwest, where there had been woodcock and nightingales, clearing the site on which Baden Powell held the first Scout camp in 1907. Within a month bracken stood a foot high out of the blackness!

That wasn't Brownsea's first fire. A worse one, in 1934, had burned half the island, leaving the trees of the west section much shorter than those of the east. It had come under fire, too, during the war when it was heavily bombed as a decoy for Holton Heath.

Once settled, I borrowed the pram dinghy from home, sharing with Richard the effort of pulling it on a pathetic little trailer from New Swanage to Redhorn Quay. Now when free I could explore all the creeks and islands. That dinghy was ideal for Poole Harbour, broad in the beam, made of light marine ply with such shallow draught that, save at very low tide, I was independent of the channels. As for tides, I learnt how quickly the shallow water withdrew from that mud. On several occasions, I had to drag the boat through mud to the nearest channel.

Now independent of the island boat and the ferry, I rowed to and fro between mainland and island, keeping a bike at Gravel Point. Stone Island lay across that route, safely underwater at high tide, well out of it when the water receded. Often, returning a little merry through the darkness and steering towards the sound of the island's peacocks, the boat grated on its pebbles. I just dragged the boat across it. The fierce tide rip out through the harbour mouth was a greater hazard. Once, happily rowing towards Gravel Point, I heard alarmed voices above, and, glancing round, saw scared faces looking down from the top of the ferry. Rowing frantically to escape the current, I avoided going under the ferry.

Long June evenings and favourable tides made it easy to explore. I followed each creek and landed on each island. Rowing around the Arne peninsula I would pull the boat up where the channel passed close to the north shore. Pools inside that stretch of beach, which were relics of clay pits, were patronised by duck. Russel Quay, once busy, long unused, stood by one such pond. There was little traffic on the river then – no roaring white motor-boats stinking of exhaust and conspicuous wealth. Up the Frome, reeds, noisy with warblers, obscured any view until sandstone Redcliff. It was four years before Ridge Wharf Yacht Centre took off. Beyond Redcliff on the Purbeck bank the houseboats began, moored there as cheap accommodation. As fortunes rose or fell those boats were abandoned, decayed. Some windows gave into a cabin of dark water. John, who grew up in Wareham, talks of Percy Westerman's barge. Writer of a very successful series of maritime novels for boys, he had moored there, retiring to it occasionally. After he died it became derelict and the sort of dangerous place kids delight in.

Up the river I would moor the dinghy by Wareham quay, stop for a drink and fish'n'chips. Sometimes I rowed on, under South Bridge and out of the tidal zone where the river, suddenly narrow and patrolled by fierce cob swans, meanders across the water-meadows. Once I nearly made it to the railway bridge before drifting back, and gazing down mesmerised at the gently-moving weed tailed back along the current, always seeking - and often seeing - large, motionless fish.

Alan Bromby had worked on Furzey Island previously, living there with his wife and two daughters. It was still owned by Lord Iliffe, who had built the house there but rarely visited it. Christine, Alan's eldest, knew the staff. So, together, we rowed over on occasion to visit. Green Island alone was deserted, and I landed several times to explore. Round and Long were smaller. Long Island had also been part of that decoy system of lights aimed to distract Nazi bombers from Holton Heath Cordite Factory. I was aware that Sir Thomas Beecham stayed on Round Island in the early fifties, because his nephew, at Hillcrest with me, gained status from the fact. I didn't know that he was there to write a biography of Delius. If the house is an eyesore, it has an unblemished view across the harbour and heath to the hills. There were other less self-confident islands to visit, such as Drove Island and Gigger's Island. Both were low but always dry land, sustaining only gorse and heather. An 18th century Mr Gigger features as a Wareham tenant of the Calcraft Estate. His family must relate somehow to the island.

Ever-expanding areas of mud become false islands which are reclaimed each year by the spread of Spartina grass. The high tide still rises among its stems but a tangle of roots make such areas safe to walk over. Spartina anglica developed in the late 19th century, when a South American variant crossed with the local cord grass. Mansel-Pleydell first found it at Ower in 1899, but, at first, it spread slowly. Once established, it accelerated. Suddenly it swathed much of the shoreline, advancing over the flats towards the channels. Recent Ordinance Survey maps recognise this reclamation, re-drawing the long-established profile of the coast.

The Frome and the Piddle, the two greatest freshwater inflows, enter the southwest corner of the harbour. The Frome forms the north border of Purbeck within which, beyond the watermeadows, there is more heathland, largely under military control. This is the final zone of Purbeck.

THE WESTERN HEATH
TO LUCKFORD LAKE

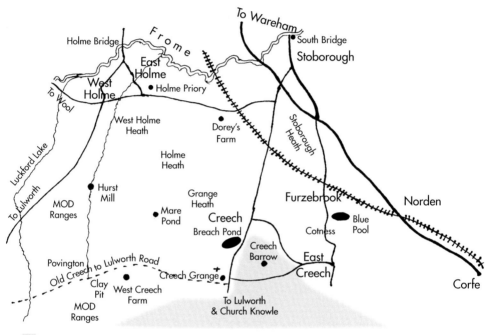

Denotes over 100 metres

The northwest of Purbeck, furthest from home, was the last tract I came to know well. My parents had friends at Furzebrook, where I took a tricycle out on the road, trapped my knee under the pedal and tore the flesh. My mother, unfazed, hastily put the bits back. For years afterwards the lines in the skin ran vertical instead of horizontal.

Furzebrook was important to us naturalists as the headquarters of the Furzebrook Research Station, which was set up in 1954 by the then Nature Conservancy. Founded in 1949, its remit was to provide scientific advice on the conservation and control of the natural flora and fauna of Great Britain, and to establish and manage nature reserves. They didn't have to go far to fulfil their task. Dr Robert Stebbings worked on the bats that had settled in the roof of their headquarters.

A little train ran from here with two sets of narrow-gauge lines crossing the Wareham road near Norden, where a road sign bore a little puffer train. A man with a red flag controlled the traffic when it passed. We always hoped for it but rarely saw it. The steam engine gave way to diesel. Then, in 1970, the line died. It carried clay and ran to Eldon siding on the main line but we took no interest in the system of tramways of which it was the sole relic.

Two rival companies dominated the clay industry. A Devon man, William Pike, started one, opening trial pits near Furzebrook in 1760. By 1791 he was producing 1,200 tons per annum. Pike Brothers was to exploit Creech, Cotness, Furzebrook, Grange, Holme and Stoborough Heaths. A London potter, Benjamin Fayle, launched the second, Fayle and Company, digging pits at Norden in 1795. Fayles grew to work Norden, Bushey, Rempstone and, later, took over the allied workings at Newton.

The early diggings were all open-cast. After the clay was dried and weathered it was transported by horse and cart to the nearest quay on the harbour and ferried to Poole. By 1796 some 10,000 tons were passing out annually through Poole's port. Apart from slumps in time of war the output has increased steadily ever since. Underground mining didn't start until a shaft was sunk at Creech in the 1890s. Then they were generally dug where the overburden was more than ten metres deep.

Fayle was first to appreciate the miraculous technical advances of his time, opening a tramway to Middlebere quay in 1806. Although still powered by horses it enormously improved efficiency, the laden trucks having a smooth, gentle downhill run. This was not strictly a railway but a plateway. The unflanged wheels were held at either side by a right-angled series of plates, set at a broad gauge of 114cm. It gave New Line Farm a name, and much of its route is now a footpath. In 1866 Pikes took the initiative, constructing an 81cm line from Furzebrook to Ridge quay and introducing its first steam locomotive, Primus. This line was extended southwest to serve new pits, including one which has now become Breach Pond. Fayle expanded eastwards, exploiting deposits at Newton, and building a new line in 1868, served by a steam locomotive, Tiny. This ran from Newton pits to Goathorn Pier. In 1905 the company opened a new line to connect Newton clayworks with Norden, making the original Middlebere line redundant. One quay was enough, and Goathorn could load small sea-going vessels. When the Wareham-Swanage line was completed in 1885 clay began to be exported through Eldon sidings and, but for Goathorn, the quays became redundant.

The Pikes and Fayles amalgamated in 1949 and the little railways were largely abandoned by 1954. Only the line crossing the Corfe-Wareham road to Eldon sidings remained, occasionally used by diesel engines until 1970. English China Clays (ECC) took over the joint company in 1968 then it was bought out by Imerys. Underground working stopped when the mine at

Norden closed in 1999. Now there are three main active diggings: the Povington pit beside West Creech Farm (the largest); Dorey's Farm pit, and that on the north of Arne peninsula.

The deserted clay-pits formed ponds, one of which is the Blue Pool. This was an early, never repeated childhood outing, and it was not the turquoise waters so much as a macaw hard by that impressed me. Enclosed by pine woodland full of fungi, its water is as rich in colour as it is poor in animal life. We soon found other claypit ponds, most of them smaller and less blue but attractive nonetheless. The works at Newton never produced any good ponds, only an interesting and uneven landscape, but there is a large one either side of the Wareham road, forming the eastern end of a heavily-dug stretch of heath running towards Creech. Beside one deserted pit, at SY939828, west of Norden Farm and near the Purbeck Way, is a wartime concrete bunker set up for the Auxillary Scouts. Other such bunkers survive in Purbeck, built to house supplies, arms and explosives for Scouts trained to sabotage behind the lines, if the Germans invaded.

In early spring we sought frogs and spawn but found toads at Breach Pond, largest of the flooded pits. Short on road sense even in a time of few cars their parchment corpses covered the nearby road. Surrounded by deciduous trees, the pond now draws anglers hoping to catch the introduced fish.

Some pits made good swimming pools, too, if you avoided feet coated with white clay, and sand martins drill their nest holes in the walls of active and derelict pits.

The Bonds, who held much of the land in the west of Purbeck, settled at Lutton more than 500 years ago. By the late 18th century, there were three branches, all descended from the late-17th century couple, John and Margaret Bond of Tyneham. Denis Bond, who lies in Steeple Church, made money: he was a lawyer and a Member of Parliament. Law, glorying in dispute and snipping a corner off every note, has bought much of Purbeck. Denis took too much, too obviously and, in 1732, was expelled from the House of Commons for fraud. But he had the loot and proceeded to expand and improve his estates. He established the three estates, buying East Holme to add to Tyneham and Creech. No heir was to own more than one estate. The principal house, Creech Grange, stands below the ridge, almost undecided whether to face east or south. The original building, held by Bindon Abbey, passed to Oliver Lawrence after the Dissolution. The 17th century house faced east. The Lawrences were staunch royalists so it was fired by Parliamentary troops in 1643. In 1681, impoverished by the Civil War, they sold Grange and, in 1691, Tyneham to the ex-republican Bonds. That must have left a bitter taste.

Around 1740 Denis Bond built the south front, cutting through the hanger-wood to gain the vista of his hilltop folly. The original 17th century façade, the present front faces east. To protect his threatened soul, he built a chapel nearby, using masonry from 12th century Holme Priory. The house was partially rebuilt in the 1840s, and thus it stands. Things have changed greatly since John W.G. Bond attained his majority in September 1886. Then, the festivities started with cricket, Grange House versus the Parish of Steeple (Steeple won), and followed with bonfires being lit on Creech Barrow, North Hill, Holme and Povington. Two months earlier, his uncle stood for election in to Parliament. 'The news that Mr Bond was elected reached Wareham at 12 o'clock, the swift-winged carrier pigeon bring the two most-welcome words "Bond In"'.

Of the three houses, the fate of Tyneham is notorious. The last owner of Creech, Ashley Bond, sold most of the estate to ECC in 1967, keeping the house until he died in 1975. Creech Grange was sold to Norman Hayward in the early 1980s. In 2004 he bought Great Wood on the hillside above. Of the three family houses only Holme Priory, with its handsome stretch of parkland, remains with the family.

Wendy Harrison (later Pushman) would tell how she was driving with her kids from there to Stoborough when an adder fell from the railway-bridge into the open-roofed car. The delinquent reptile had to be flicked out with a stick. I always give an involuntary glance up at that bridge. Until motorised we saw little beyond Grange. All my friends became interested in cars, took their driving tests and passed. In 1961 I bought a moped, followed by a series of motorbikes. Suddenly the large tract of army-controlled heathland lay open to us. We christened it Red Cow Country from the rough red cattle that grazed there.

One June evening in the mid 1970s when IRA terrorism was at its peak Trev and I parked along Holme Lane, looked left and right along the road, jumped a gate and, full of seasonal *joie de vivre*, ran off along a ride. Cuckoos called; the evening was beautiful, and, in the distance, someone was shooting rabbits. As dusk gathered, we regained the road further along and walked back along it to find the car surrounded by blue flashing lights. Someone had reported two men chasing each other into the army ranges - followed by shots.

Most outings were less eventful. The untended area was rich in wildlife, ranging from less common butterflies, such as white admirals, to frogs (because farmers sprayed with gay abandon, they were a rarity elsewhere), to various birds uniquely settled in the shelter of the guns. We came on the only curlew's nest I've seen and a nightjar's nest. Owls and kestrels lived in the ruined farm buildings, and the area had the densest population of nightingales in Purbeck. Once we even got permission to visit the area with the eminent ornithologist Horace Alexander and were posed with the problem of guiding our army guide through places we already knew. If he

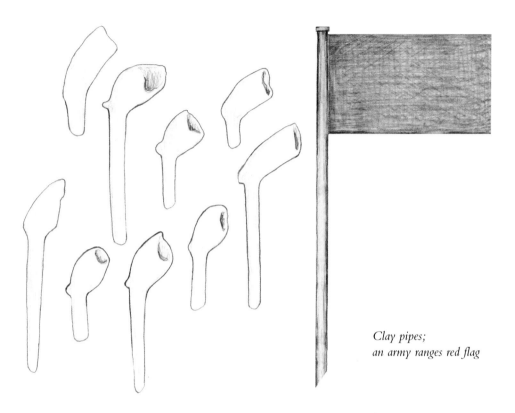

Clay pipes;
an army ranges red flag

was impressed by our ability to turn up nests he gave no indication. Horace had been a friend since the late '50s. An exact contemporary of Adolf Hitler, his life confounded astrology. A quaker, he had been a concientious objector in WW1. He met Mahatma Gandhi in 1929 and became an admirer of his passive action. When the classic *Handbook of British Birds* was produced he was responsible for compiling the birdsong charts. A sickly child, he died in Pennsylvania in 1989 aged 100.

We explored along Luckford Lake, the little stream that forms much of Purbeck's western border, as it runs through thickets busy with families of small birds. We saw Hurst Mill, an isolated feature on many old maps, fall to ruin beside the largest stream to cross this stretch of heath. There an outbuilding where hay had been stored always seemed to offer a healthy crop of mushrooms.

I had seen the flashes by night, sometimes seen firing by day: 'Reaching Wareham...I bought a hot pie and sat by the river eating it...They were firing on the army range and I could see shells hitting the side of the hill (in Red

Cow Country)...' I was never actually under fire but friends had been. One summer evening, having parked at Creech, John and I followed the old road straight across the range to East Lulworth, stopping at the Weld Arms for a pint. As we drank a downpour and a barrage of guns broke almost simultaneously. Luckily it was not too late to call his father out, and cadge a lift back to the car. Another time a helicopter came in low and landed in an open area where, becoming blasé, I had been collecting mushrooms. I hid. They took off, advancing in an ever-increasing circle about the place. When they were distant I ran like hell, irrespective of brambles or bog, ducking into undergrowth when they approached. Blood flowing, I gained the wood with clothes torn and thick with black mud.

Those who eked a living from this poor acid soil were called 'heathcroppers'. Their life was tough. The patch of land they cleared for vegetables or crops was invaded by bracken and gorse and their cattle found mean grazing. The heathland was always thinly-populated, the nearest thing to a village being Povington, a farm and several homesteads loosely gathered. Only the fields nearest to the chalk ridge were productive. Most of the farm-buildings stood derelict as they had been left in 1943 although some still stored fodder and straw as they fell into ruin. There were wrecked cottages of cob, walls of clay consolidated with straw and gravel. At each dead homestead some vestige of cultivation would reveal itself in spring - always daffodils, the pink blossom of a sad apple tree, or a rose amongst brambles. Does the wooden granary at West Creech Farm still perch on its staddle stones?

★

In the early 19th century, some folk had the leisure and skill to keep diaries. John Bond of Creech wrote a notebook, with killings punctuating most pages. The keeper traps a polecat of 'amazing size', and slays the young peregrines on Gad Cliff. There are regular September records of land rails (corncrakes), shot on migration. He even claims one for December 1839. But it was mechanised farming, not his like, that drove them from Britain. He includes occasional nature notes. In the 1820s a man brought brent geese shot off Brownsea Island to sell. In December 1832 he records picking up many stormy petrels on the hillside - true ocean birds blown far inland (similarly, a Leach's petrel turned up on the path at Dunshay several years ago). Then: 'June 1842. Glow Worms: Very hot and sultry, windows open - Candles lighted many of these insects flew about the room - they were small with four wings and luminous appearance in the tail.' That has puzzled me. The glowing female glow-worm is flightless. Were they flying males, which occasionally light up, or fireflies blown across the Channel by freak weather?

19-year-old Thomas Bartlett of Wareham started a gamebook in December 1807 by listing the contents of the larder: '1 pheasant, 3½ couple of wildfowl, 7½ couple Snipes, 2 couple Water Rail, 1 Moorhen, 5 partridges,

1 hare, 1 Rabit, 11 lobsters, 1 Codfish, 2 Starlings.' In 1808 he met soldiers of the 53rd Regiment of Foot, many of them Germans, marching towards Kent. Some of their officers stayed nearby and he went shooting near Stoborough with General Linsingen who, at 82, impressed him by killing with every shot. Some outings were less fortunate, as in November 1808: 'At 12 o'clock went to Stoborough stay here half past one killed two Snipes. Bill fell into a Ditch over head and Ears.'

Fish feature, too. He records stocking their new pond 'above Bacon's Mill'. 'We hired a cart to go to Smedmore to fetch Carp ... I breakfasted with Mr Clavell after breakfast we went to the Pond, and two men got into it up to their middles in mud, and took out between 70 and 80 brace with their hands.' They loaded these into a hogshead on the cart, and Bartlett set off via Grange, where he changed the water. Half the fish survived to be put into the pond. But the grid between it and the river proved too wide and in the night they all swam away. A fortnight later he repeated the journey, dining with Mr Clavell and coming back with half as many fish. Only two died. The river was well stocked in those days: 'with a net to Holme Bridge; caught in an hour and a half about 300 brace of Roach; forty brace very large and eleven brace Jack 4 brace very fine and large.' Luckford Lake joins the Frome above Holme Bridge after running parallel across the water-meadows. The meandering river tried to swallow its lower reaches but fishermen reinforced the bank to keep the two apart. When the Freshwater Laboratories acquired the land their policy was to let nature take its course. The river duly ate through the bank around 1997, adding a little strip of land to Purbeck!

Holme Bridge replaced a ford, probably the Luck Ford of Luckford Lake, as one of two crossings of the Frome into Purbeck. The other is South Bridge in Wareham, described in 1882 as 'leaning noticeably to the east'; it was demolished in 1926. Foundations of a mediaeval predecessor were found during rebuilding. The old bridge and its datestone went to Trigon House where the date 1788 now graces a garage doorway. Although there has been a bridge at Holme since the 13th century the present structure dates from the 16th century and has been much patched over the years. It was the site of a heroic defence in 1643 when a small force of royalists held back 300 Parliamentary troops, their two injured officers being propped up against the parapet to encourage their men. The lieutenant died. During the Second World War the army put up a Bailey Bridge alongside the old one so that their tanks could pass to and fro, but normal traffic was supposed to keep to the old bridge. A modern bridge was built just downstream in 1963, by-passing the old one but leaving it in place.

There are two hamlets at Holme. Across a little ford East Holme centres on an old barn and a restored granary perched on twelve staddle stones. Holme Priory, a farm house converted by Nathaniel Bond (the first of four

Nathaniel Bonds to own it) into a modest country seat in the 1760s, stands on its eastern edge looking south across meadow with some magnificent trees. The original, small pre-Reformation priory succumbed to the Dissolution, but the church served the community until 1715, and was demolished in 1746. In 1881 the Priory was let until Martin Bond settled there in 1955. His son currently holds it. Beyond the house is the little church of St John the Evangelist.

In 1864 the current Nathaniel married Lady Selina Scott of Encombe. Selina was well thought of. Even Mrs Panton is generous in her praise. They built the church the following year, Selina herself painting the texts and creeper decoration. The architect John Hicks of Dorchester achieved fame by employing Thomas Hardy in his office for six years. The outer walls are of sandstone quarried from Holme Mount on the estate, surviving better than the Purbeck marble used for shafts and altar steps.

West Holme's modern fame came when James Goldsack launched a 'Pick Your Own' project in 1978 with strawberries, after shelling out on an expensive irrigator two years earlier to combat the drought. It soon became popular and people turned up on me with their strawberries or raspberries. He shifted from rented land to their own present site in 1985 and in 1991 his son, Simon, started his flourishing Holme Nurseries.

They took me out onto the water meadows to see where Luckford Lake had been captured. Above the tidal reach the Frome meanders artfully in hairpin curves across the deep green of its water meadows. I learned that the meadows were divided into 'lawnes' from which certain folk, not necessarily tenants, had right to harvest hay. A project to mark fish here had revealed that dace would wander up to 400m from the river to feed through the flooded grass, and then return to the river. A Messerschmitt 110, shot down by fighters, crashed by the river east of the bridge in August 1940, embedding itself deep in the mud. Mr Barnes, the farmer of Priory Farm, took the cockpit cover as a cloche. The rest of the plane lay there until it was dug out some 20 years ago.

Long manes of weed waved gently on the current and a kingfisher warned of its passing with a shrill 'peep'. Downstream, Holme Bridge (the new one - not the old) opened onto the mainland, onto the busy A342 between Bournemouth and Dorchester. In Purbeck the traffic just snarls. There it roars.

Mortons House Hotel

East Street Corfe Castle Dorset BH20 5EE   01929 480988

ETC 3 Star Silver Award – AA 3 Star 77% - 2 AA Rosette Restaurant

Morning Coffee – Lunches
– Afternoon and Cream Teas – Evening Meals
Civil Wedding License – Private Functions & Conference Facilities
Built in the shape of an 'E' to commemorate Elizabeth 1 with stone
taken from the 'sleighted' castle, Mortons House Hotel boasts a fine
reputation for service, and for culinary excellence, with an award
winning Two AA rosette restaurant.

Corfe Castle, the old fairytale capital of the 'Isle of Purbeck' is a
beautiful part of this corner of England, steeped in history and a
designated area of outstanding natural beauty, the World Heritage
Coastline also dominates the scene.

Cliff top walks, beaches, museums, stately homes, golf courses,
and endless opportunities await visitors.

All of the 19 ensuite bedrooms are have been tastefully decorated and
furnished. Suites, Character rooms, and those with Castle views available.

The hotel is privately owned and run by two families and
is "accessible to all"

Beavers

'Beavers is a child-friendly, doggy-friendly family restaurant set in the heart of the Jurassic Coast.'

'We have a wide and varied menu including breakfast, lunch and dinner; great wines, draught lager and traditional cream teas.'

'During the summer months we open 9am to 9pm and close at 5pm during the winter.'

14 Institute Road, Swanage Tel: 01929 427292

BURDEN BUILDING SERVICES LTD

All types of Building Work undertaken

*All types of building work
undertaken
Competitive rates
Free Estimates*

Happy to support the local community

"Newfoundlands"
Newfoundlands Close
Worth Matravers
Swanage
Dorset

Tel/Fax: 01929 439209
Mobile: 07966 216288

Achieve Qualifications Online
National Vocational Qualifications

Beauty, Holistic therapies and Nail technique NVQ's

Do work and family commitments prevent you from attending a full/part time course?
Do you need a flexible approach to study?

- Regular course start dates
- Onlline delivery via our learning website for the theory and tutorial support
- Plus Saturday or Sunday workshops for each practical subject
- Qualified lecturers and subject specialists deiver the courses

For information regarding courses, prices, start dates and modes of study please contact us.

Fully supported, totally flexible, off the shelf units of study
EDEXCEL approved

Website: www.connect2beauty.co.uk
Email: info@vocationonline.co.uk
Tel: 07981356730

PURBECK STONE CONSTRUCTION
Stone supplied and fixed by

THE STONE WORK SPECIALIST
Patios - Porches - Fireplaces - Walls, etc

"Wishing St George's School
many happy years to come"

Ross Prior, 'Cosy Corner',
Off Haycrafts Lane,
Harmans Cross, Swanage.
Telephone: 481217

The MKL Partnership
Chartered Certified Accountants

Herston Cross House, 230 High Street, Swanage

Tax and VAT   PAYE bureau
Self-assessment - Personal and Corporate
Accountancy and Book-Keeping Services
Cash-flows and Projections

For a confidential FREE initial consultation with Mike or Kevin to discuss your tax or accountancy affairs, telephone the number below. There is no obligation.

Why face the hassle of driving to, and parking in, Poole or Bournemouth, when we have easy, free parking?

Why pay large town fees? We have low overheads and reflect this in our charges. Visits and evening appointments by arrangement.

SWANAGE 425552 Fax: 01929 426628
E-Mail: mail@mklp.co.uk www.MKLP.co.uk